You Are God Alone

DR. MARY J. BRYANT

Kingdom Builders Publications LLC

You are God Alone

© 2019 Dr. Mary J. Bryant
You Are God Alone
Kingdom Builders Publications, LLC

All rights reserved. No part of this book may be reproduced or transmitted in any form or by any means without written permission from the author.

Printed in the USA

ISBN
978-0-578-57923-8

Authored by
Dr. Mary J. Bryant

Editors
Prophetess Marilyn Dozier
Kingdom Builders Publications

Cover Design
Dr. Mary J. Bryant

Scriptures on the cover
Isaiah 43:10c The Voce Bible Copyright © 2012 Thomas Nelson, Inc. The Voice™ translation © 2012 Ecclesia Bible Society All rights reserved.
Psalm 48:14 New International Version (NIV) Holy Bible, New International Version®, NIV® Copyright © 1973, 1978, 1984, 2011 by Biblica, Inc. ® Used by permission. All rights reserved worldwide.
Scripture quoted by permission. Quotations designated (NET) are from the NET Bible® copyright ©1996-2016 by Biblical Studies Press, L.L.C. http://netbible.com All rights reserved.

The names: THE NET BIBLE®, NEW ENGLISH TRANSLATION COPYRIGHT © 1996 BY BIBLICAL STUDIES PRESS, L.L.C. NET Bible® IS A REGISTERED TRADEMARK THE NET BIBLE® LOGO, SERVICE MARK COPYRIGHT © 1997 BY BIBLICAL STUDIES PRESS, L.L.C. ALL RIGHTS RESERVED
SATELLITE IMAGERY COPYRIGHT © RØHR PRODUCTIONS LTD. AND CENTRE NATIONAL D'ÉTUDES SPATIALES PHOTOGRAPHS COPYRIGHT ©) RØHR PRODUCTIONS LTD.
The Complete Jewish Bible

Copyright and Usage Information
According to the information we have received, this translation of the Holy Bible is in the public domain, since its copyright has expired. Feel free to use as you wish.

Dr. Bryant is available for Teaching and Speaking opportunities

Please contact

doveministry378@yahoo.com

Watch her Faith In Action Podcast on
www.YouTube.com - Mary J. Bryant Faith in Action

Visit the website:
www.doveministry378.org

Phone:
(803) 409-9368

You are God Alone

Psalm 46:8-11 (The Passion Translation)

Everyone look! Come and see the breathtaking wonders of our God. For he brings both ruin and revival. And he's the One who makes conflicts to end throughout the earth, breaking and burning every weapon of war. Surrender your anxiety! Be silent and stop your striving and you will see that I am God. I am the God above all the nations and I will be exalted throughout the whole earth. Here he stands! The Commander! The Mighty Lord of Angel-Armies is on our side! The God of Jacob fights for us

You are God Alone
This Book Belongs to

_____

"For God so loved the world he gave his only begotten Son that whosoever believeth should not perish but have everlasting life."
John 3:16

God – The Greatest Person

So Loved – The Greatest Devotion

The World – The Greatest Number

He Gave – The Greatest Act

His Only Begotten Son – The Greatest Gift

That Whosoever Believeth – The Greatest Condition

Should Not Perish – The Greatest Mercy

Have Everlasting Life – The Greatest Result

TABLE OF CONTENTS

DEDICATION PAGE	VIII
ACKNOWLEDGMENTS	X
PRAYER	XI
FOREWORD	XII
INTRODUCTION	XIV
NAMES OF GOD	17
GOD CREATOR	20
ATTRIBUTES OF GOD	27
GOD IS LOVE	37
THE TRINITY: GOD FATHER, GOD SON, GOD HOLY SPIRIT	41
GOD THE SON: GOD BESIDE	46
GOD THE HOLY SPIRIT: GOD WITHIN	51
KNOWING GOD	57
THE WORD OF GOD	61
GOD IN THE PSALMS	66
THE WRATH OF GOD: PROVOKING GOD TO ANGER	74
THE GOODNESS OF GOD	83
THE DUTY OF MAN TO GOD	87
LIFE WITHOUT GOD	89
GOD'S KINGDOM	92
GOD'S HEART FOR THE WORLD	96
CHOOSE GOD AND LIVE: THE CHOICE IS YOURS	101
CONCLUSION	105
FROM THE AUTHOR	107

You are God Alone

You are God Alone

DEDICATION PAGE

This book is dedicated to the One who has inspired me and helped to become a published author. I give glory, honor, and praise to Him. To God, the blessed and Only Ruler, the King of kings and Lord of lords,

Who alone is immortal and lives in unapproachable light, whom no one has seen or can see. To Him be honor and might forever. Amen!
(1st Timothy 6:14)

I'm thanking you, God, from a full heart, I'm writing the book on your wonders. I'm whistling, laughing, and jumping for joy; I'm singing your song, High God. (Psalm 9:1-2 MSG)

ACKNOWLEDGMENTS

I once again acknowledge my wonderful family: my husband **Michael**; our children: **Michael, Megan,** and **Marquis** and our granddaughter, **Michaela Jayne Grace**. I thank God for them. I thank each of them for their continued support.

I acknowledge **Prophetess Marilyn Dozer** for providing her editing service for this book project. I thank God for her willingness and eagerness to be a part of this project.

I acknowledge **Prophet Shirley Ford** for providing the forward for this book. She didn't hesitate in saying "yes" when I was led to ask her to provide the forward. She holds a very special place in my heart for all her of support and encouragement over the years.

I also want to acknowledge everyone who will support this book project. I appreciate them and pray God's blessings for their life.

Last but certainly not least to **Louise Smith**. Thank you from the bottom of my heart.

A Big Shout Out to my **Scotia family**. I love you beyond the moon…

PSS: A shout out to **Homer Bridges** (I told you I would mention you in one of my books.)

Prayer

Heavenly Father, I come to You on behalf of those who will read this book. I pray that they learn to trust You and they open their hearts to You to get to know You in all Your majesty and awe. Give them a hunger and thirst for Your righteousness and they will diligently seek You like never before.

I pray that those who read this book will be given the Spirit of wisdom and revelation and that the eyes of their hearts be enlightened in order that they may know the hope to which You have called them.

I pray that Jesus Christ dwell in their hearts by faith that they be rooted and grounded in love. May they know the love of Christ that passes all knowledge and be filled with the fullness of God.

Father, I pray that they may walk worthy of the Lord. May they be fruitful in every good work and always increasing in the knowledge of God. Fill them Father with the knowledge of Your will in all wisdom and spiritual understanding.

May the God of peace equip you with everything good for doing His will and may He work in us what is pleasing to Him through Christ Jesus. (Hebrews 13:20-24). In Jesus Christ Mighty Name I do pray. Amen.

Confession:
I belong to God and I will do the will of God from my heart.

FOREWORD

"Always be prepared to give an answer to everyone for the hope that you have." 1st Peter 3:15

The hope that Dr. Mary J. Bryant has written in YOU ARE GOD ALONE is a beautiful masterpiece for all believers. As Dr. Bryant takes the reader into the heart and mind of our heavenly Father, God's unfailing love for us is so eloquently revealed. She conveys to the reader exactly who God is and the undisputable fact that He is God alone. This masterpiece will admonish you to get to know our heavenly Father more intimately. The more you know about our Father through Jesus Christ the more you will want to know Him.

I really could not stop reading about the awesomeness of our Father. A reminder of who He is. How He sent His only begotten Son to pay our sin debt. Dr. Bryant takes the reader into the Word of God with all of its truth, declarations, experiences, and examples by the leading of the Holy Spirit. The reader's spirit will be united with her as the Word of God is spoken throughout the pages. YOU ARE GOD ALONE is for the mature Christian/Believer of Christ and for the Babe in Christ. I do believe that it will even lead the unsaved to receive the awesome free gift of salvation.

This quote by Dr. Bryant really stood out to me: "Once we know and believe that God is Creator of everything that knowledge should shape the way we think, the way we live, the way we love, and guard our activities." **Glory to God**! As I read page fifteen, the Spirit of the Lord came upon me. Dr. Bryant, so powerfully, gives us the finding of the attributes of God, the incomparable attributes of God. What a joyful experience I encountered.

This masterpiece that Dr. Bryant has written will stir the Believer to love God even more. The unsaved has the perfect illustration of salvation given on page thirty-five. The value of this book, YOU ARE GOD ALONE, will become priceless to all who reads it. I am a witness because it has blessed me down in my soul. I challenge you to open your heart and soul to receive a fresh breath from YOU ARE GOD ALONE.

Thank you, Dr. Bryant, for giving me the opportunity to read and write the forward for this masterpiece, YOU ARE GOD ALONE.

God Bless you,
Prophet Shirley E. Ford
Rehoboth Restoration Church
Columbia, South Carolina

INTRODUCTION

When I started my journey in becoming a published author, it was with my relationship with Jesus in view. My first book is titled Prayers, Poems, and Precious Moments. Then the inspiration came for my second book, I Recommend Jesus. The third inspirational book again came by inspiration entitled New Life in Christ by Faith. But let also mention that I was also given favor to publish children's book, Marquis Finds a Friend and Marquis Goes to the Circus, with a third one on the way: Marquis Gets a Bicycle for Christmas.

Now I present to you the fourth inspirational book, You are God Alone. The Bible teaches that He is both God is and God alone. God is the eternal God who created a universe of space and time, because God created heaven and earth and everything in it (Psalm 24:1; 1st Corinthians 10:26). That means ALL; nothing or no one is left out. He reigns over the earth, and there He accomplishes His purposes. God is defined as the Supreme Being.

The purpose of this work is to help open the door to know God in a more intimate way. It is my prayer that each person will learn (all the more) that God is Spirit and God is absolute in His being. Additionally, that each person will understand that God has personality and God's basic attribute is holiness and from holiness flows His love, mercy, and grace. It is God who sent His Son to reveal Himself to humanity (John 1:18). Thus, apart from the revelation and the illumination of the Holy Spirit the message will not be believed or understood.

It is in Genesis that we get a glimpse of God's original intent for us and how we were meant to relate to Him, to each other, and to our world. God created us in His image, His likeness, and we were created to carry out His work in the earth. Through His written word, God has given us the basic plan to know and understand how to serve Him.

Genesis also begins to reveal the nature and character of God. God has no beginning and no end. Truthfully, He is the beginning and the end, Alpha and Omega. He has always been and always will be. He is known as Elohim (Father, Son, and Holy Spirit).

It is in God's Word that we realize our sin and His Word convicts us of sin. It is His Word that helps cleanse us from the pollution of sin. His Word imparts strength and instructs us in what we are to do. God's Word provides us with a sword for victory over sin and makes us fruitful while giving us power to pray.

God earnestly wants us to attain personal knowledge of Him. However, while God can be known, there is always more to be learned about Him. Scriptures teaches that the knowledge of God is "too wonderful" (Psalm 139:6); "unsearchable (Psalm 145:3); and "infinite" (Psalm 147:5). The Bible also teaches that we cannot know God personally apart from His Word. To know God personally is to be saved and have eternal life. In other words, the Scriptures and the Gospel contain the part that brings mankind to know God in three very important ways. (1) the gospel is the agent of the new birth (James 1:18); (2) it is like the implanted seed without which the conception of new life cannot occur and a cleansing agent for the sinner who believes that gets washed resulting in salvation (Ephesians 5:26); and (3) the scriptures are like a teacher bringing the wisdom that leads to salvation (2nd Timothy 3:15).

As wonderful as it is to be saved for all eternity, it is my desire for us to long to walk with the Lord today. We need to hear His voice, know His heart, and receive His gifts to participate in what He is doing now. It is my prayer that as believers, we depend strongly on God and His Word. May this work help us to cultivate a deeper relationship with God (Father, Son, and Holy Spirit). The Lord is our God. We must love Him with our whole mind, our whole being, and all our strength (Deuteronomy 6:4-5). We become intimate with God as we talk with Him in prayer and study His Word. The more we know God, the more we love Him and want to respond to His desires for our lives. We approach life according to His perspective. This choice is based on faith that says He is God and God alone.

NAMES OF GOD
Chapter One

I believe that we have been given the many names of God to help us to learn His character. So, it is vitally important for each of us to understand those names; because each name reveals something wonderful and awesome of His Sovereign character. These names also show us the diversities of how God helps each one of us in our times of need. As we read the Bible, we will see how God reveals a new name each time the people either face a greed need or when God come through and provide a blessing in such a supernatural way.

For example, Abraham, Isaac, and Jacob knew God as God Almighty because they needed His might power to protect them from their enemies. Moses and the children of Israel, on the other hand, learned that God was Lord, master over every nation and everything. As God delivered them from Pharaoh, the most powerful ruler in the world, and brought them into the Promised Land, they came to experience Him as Lord, preeminently powerful over the pagan gods of their day. When we are grieving, He is revealed as our Comforter. When we are in need, He is revealed as our Provider. When we are sick, He is revealed as our Healer. When we are in trouble, He is revealed as Shield and Strength.

I encourage you to get into a personal relationship with God the Father through Jesus Christ because without that direct personal fellowship only learn about God without growing to really know Him. I have listed some of the names of God to get you started in the process of knowing God as the Father.

ELOHIM (God) (**Genesis 1:1**)

In the beginning Elohim (God) created the heaven and the earth

LORD God (**Genesis 2:4**)

There are the generations of the heavens and of the earth when they were created, in the day that the LORD God made the earth and the heavens

Most High God (**Genesis 14:18-22**)

And Melchizedek king of Salem brought forth bread and wine: and he was the priest of the Most High God.

And he blessed him, and said, Blessed be Abram of the most high God, possessor of heaven and earth:

And blessed be the Most High God, which hath delivered thine enemies into thy hand. And he gave him tithes of all.

And the king of Sodom said unto Abram, give me the person, and take the goods to thyself.

And Abram said to the king of Sodom, I have lift up mine hand unto the LORD, the Most High God, the possessor of heaven and earth,

- ❖ Almighty God (**Genesis 17:1-2**)
- ❖ Everlasting God (**Genesis 21:33**)
- ❖ God Almighty (**Genesis 28:3**)
- ❖ I Am (Exodus 3:14)
- ❖ Yahweh (**Exodus 6:3**)
- ❖ Jealous (Exodus 34:14)
- ❖ Eternal God (Deuteronomy 33:27)
- ❖ Living God (**Joshua 3:10**)

- ❖ God of Hosts (**Psalm 80:7**)
- ❖ Lord of Hosts (**Isaiah 1:24**)
- ❖ Holy One of Israel (**Isaiah 43:3, 14, 15**)
- ❖ Mighty God (Jeremiah 32:187)
- ❖ God of Heaven (**Jonah 1:9**)
- ❖ Heavenly Father (**Matthew 6:26**)
- ❖ King Eternal (1ˢᵗ Timothy 1:17)
- ❖ Only Potentate (**1ˢᵗ Timothy 6:15**)
- ❖ Father of Lights (**James 1:17**)

GOD CREATOR
Chapter Two

"In the beginning God created the heavens and the earth."
(Genesis 1:1, NIV)

Though God is present from the first words in the Bible, He is eternal and exists outside of time. God in Christ is Creator and Lord (Genesis 1:31; Colossians 1:16-17). God's creation runs from Genesis to Revelation, from the original creation of the heavens and the earth to the creation of a new heaven and earth (Revelation 21:1).

God's initial work was *"good"* (Genesis 1:4, 10, 12, 18,21,25) and *"very good"* (1:31). Though sin came, God's work did not end with Adam and Eve. In fact, Genesis is not so much the origin of history of humanity as it is the first chapter in the history of the redemption of mankind. He continues in His redemption by providing for us and sustaining for us. God continually works to bring people into a saving relationship with Him through the shed Blood of Jesus Christ.

As we give God thanks for saving us from sin, we should also thank Him for creating us also. He is our powerful Creator and Compassionate Savior. Once we have put our faith in the Work of God's Son Jesus Christ and received salvation, there is so much more of God to experience. God can accomplish a life changing transformation for all who truly believe in Christ. Our conversion and regeneration are merely the start of a lifelong spiritual journey with Him. We are to desire to know more and more about who He is and who we are. We are given understanding of how to live our lives in honor of the Creator. In order to receive that understanding we must get to know Him as Creator.

As Creator, He has created each of us unique. King David wrote in

Psalm 139 expressions of this fundamental truth. Though we have many things in common, God has created us to be one of a kind. That means no one else has the same make up as you and I. God in His infinite wisdom and power has given no two person the same fingerprints. He knows each one of intimately and uniquely. Scripture tells us the even the hairs on our head our numbered (Matthew 10:30; Luke 12:7). Each of us has been created by God for special reasons. Ephesians 2:10 tells us we have been created for "good works" as "masterpieces" before the foundation of the world. God already counted us worthy before we were ever born and assigned us to do good works according to His good pleasure.

God, the Creator has brought everything into being (Psalm 146:6; 148:5). He sustains the world and its creatures with intimate care (Psalm 147:4-5). He provides water (147:8, 16, 17). He provides food and nourishment (145:15, 16; 147:14). He rules creation throughout eternity (146:10; 148:6). The Prophet Isaiah wrote in chapter 40-

"Who hath measured the waters in the hollow of his hand meted (measured) out heaven with the span, and comprehended the dust of the earth in a measure, and weighted the mountains in scales, and the hills in a balance? Who hath directed the Spirit (Holy Spirit) of the LORD, or being his counsellor hath taught him? With whom took he counsel, and who instructed him, and taught him in the path of judgment, and taught him knowledge, and shewed to him the way of understanding?" (12—14 KJV)

Who can we compare our God and Creator to? What image is like Him? He is the Eternal God that sits above the circle of the earth and we are like grasshoppers. His hands stretched out the heavens like a cover. No one is His equal; He is Elohim. He says of Himself in Isaiah 43:13 – "Yea, before the day was, I am he; and there is none that can deliver out of my hand: I will work, and who shall let it?" He is the Creator who can do a new thing; make a way in the wilderness, and rivers in the desert (Isaiah 43:1).

God is to be praised as Creator. He is to be trusted as sovereign LORD. He has an eternal plan that covers all events and destinies without exception, and with power to redeem, re-create and renew. Proverbs 16:4 teaches, "The LORD has made everything for his own purposes, even the wicked for a day of disaster" (NLT). It is an awesome revelation to realize that we trust the Almighty Creator and moment by moment we depend on God the Creator for our very existence. Thus, we live lives of devotion, commitment, gratefulness, and loyalty toward an Awesome and Majestic God.

> " ¹*Come, let us sing for joy to the LORD; let us shout aloud to the Rock of our salvation.*
>
> *²Let us come before him with thanksgiving and extol him with music and song.*
>
> *³For the LORD is the great God, the great King above all gods.*
>
> *⁴In his hand are the depths of the earth, and the mountain peaks belong to him.*
>
> *⁵The sea is his, for he made it and his hands formed the dry land.*
>
> *⁶Come, let us bow down in worship, let us kneel before the* LORD **our Maker;**
>
> *⁷for he is our God and we are the people of his pasture, the flock under his care."*
> *(Psalm 95:1-7)*

God reveals Himself by His written revelation, the Bible and the evidence of creation because God created all things through His Son, Jesus (Ephesians 3:9). The evidence of an all-powerful Creator and many of His attributes are clearly seen by those who are willing to see.

Romans 1:20-21 teaches, *"For since the creation of the world God's invisible qualities—his eternal power and divine nature—have been clearly seen, being understood from what has been made, so that people are without excuse."* Once we know and believe that God is Creator of everything, that knowledge should shape the way we think, the way we live, the way we love and guide our actions. The question to ask oneself is, "Is my life glorifying God as my Creator?" "For although they knew God, they neither glorified him as God nor gave thanks to him, but their thinking became futile and their foolish hearts were darkened." Romans 1:21

I will conclude with a magnificent poem of creation found in Isaiah 40:12-15, 21-31.

> *¹²Who has measured the waters in the hollow of his hand,*
> *or with the breadth of his hand marked off the heavens?*
> *Who has held the dust of the earth in a basket,*
> *or weighed the mountains on the scales*
> *and the hills in a balance?*
> *¹³Who has understood the mind of the LORD,*
> *or instructed him as his counselor?*
> *¹⁴Whom did the LORD consult to enlighten him,*
> *and who taught him the right way?*
> *¹⁵Who was it that taught him knowledge*
> *or showed him the path of understanding? ....*
>
> *²¹Do you not know?*
> *Have you not heard?*
> *Has it not been told you from the beginning?*
> *Have you not understood since the earth was founded?*
> *²²He sits enthroned above the circle of the earth,*
> *and its people are like grasshoppers.*
> *He stretches out the heavens like a canopy, and spreads them out like a tent*
> *to live in.*

²³He brings princes to naught
and reduces the rulers of this world to nothing.
²⁴No sooner are they planted,
no sooner are they sown,
no sooner do they take root in the ground,
than he blows on them and they wither,
and a whirlwind sweeps them away like chaff.
²⁵"To whom will you compare me?
Or who is my equal?" says the Holy One.
²⁶Lift your eyes and look to the heavens:
Who created all these?
He who brings out the starry host one by one,
and calls them each by name.
Because of his great power and mighty strength,
not one of them is missing.
²⁷Why do you say, O Jacob,
and complain, O Israel,
"My way is hidden from the LORD;
my cause is disregarded by my God"?
²⁸Do you not know?
Have you not heard?
The LORD is the everlasting God
the **Creator of the ends of the earth.**
He will not grow tired or weary,
and his understanding no one can fathom.
²⁹He gives strength to the weary
and increases the power of the weak.
³⁰Even youths grow tired and weary,
and young men stumble and fall;
³¹but those who hope in the LORD
will renew their strength.

*They will soar on wings like eagles;
they will run and not grow weary,
they will walk and not be faint.*

You are God Alone

Prayer

Father, thank you for having a chance to get to know You as our Creator. Help us to always keep ourselves in the right perspective, that we are the created ones and You are the Creator. Thank you for life in your image. In Jesus' name, we pray. Amen.

Job 12:10-16 New International Version (NIV)

ATTRIBUTES OF GOD
Chapter Three

There are two truths the Bible teaches us concerning the knowledge of God. It teaches us that God is incomprehensible and knowable. To say God is incomprehensible, simply lets us know that God is infinite. **Psalm 147:5** states, "Great is our Lord, and mighty in power; His understanding is infinite." We cannot know everything there is to know about Him because we are finite beings. Yet on the other hand, God is knowable because we can grow in the grace and knowledge of who He is. We can, indeed, have a personal and growing relationship with Him. We can comprehend information revealed about God.

What does it mean when I talk about the attributes of God? Well, simply put, I am talking about the nature of God, who God is in His manifested character. The Bible teaches us something that is true about God or it shows what is true about God. I would like to look at several of God's awesome attributes.

God is Incomparable. In 2nd **Samuel 7:22-24 (MSG)**, we read: "This is what makes you so great, Master God! There is none like you, no God but you, nothing to compare with what we've heard with our own ears." **Exodus 15:11** reads: "Who compares with you among gods of God? Who compares with you in power, in holy majesty, in awesome praises, wonder-working God?" Thus, the title of this book: God is God Alone!

I can go on and on! Although we are created in the image and likeness of God, we cannot compare to His Greatness, His Power, His Majesty, or His Knowledge. He is unequaled and perfect. He is incomparable because He is the Potter and we are the clay. He knows the past, present, and future, including what we are thinking at any given moment. Yes, He declares the end from the beginning (**Isaiah 46:8-10**).

God is incomparable because He is independent of, above, and distinct from this universe. He is outside, above, and before this time-space universe. He is "I Am that I Am". He is different and independent from all His creation. He does not need us to exist but we need Him to exist. God is self-existent (Exodus 3:14; Psalm 90:2; Romans 11:36; 1st Corinthians 8:6; Colossians 1:16-17). He infinitely greater and higher than the created order (1st Kings 8:27; Isaiah 66: 1-2; Acts 17: 24-25).

God is unequaled. Isaiah 40:25 asks the question, "To whom then will ye liken me, or shall I be equal? saith the Holy One." This fortieth chapter of Isaiah really lays out the God of this universe and sets Him apart and far above His creation. He asks a number of questions. In verse 12, the question is asked, "Who hath measured the waters in the hollow of his hand, and measured out heaven with the span, and comprehended the dust of the earth in a measure, and weighted the mountains in scales, and the hills in a balance?" In verse 13, "Who hath directed the Holy Spirit of the LORD, or being his counsellor hath taught him?" Verse 14, "With whom took he counsel, and who instructed him, and taught him in the path of judgment, and taught him knowledge, and shewed to him the way of understanding?" Then after letting us know that even the nations areas a drop in the bucket and as the small dust of the balance. All nations before him is nothing. Then verse 18 asks, "To whom then will ye liken God? Or what likeness will ye compare unto him?"

God is unequaled because He exists independently of any cause. God exists from Himself. He has always existed and will always exist. No one or nothing has caused God's existence and no one or nothing can make it to cease. He is eternal, without beginning or end. He declares the end from the beginning and from ancient times things which have not been done, Saying, 'My purpose will be established, and I will accomplish all My good pleasure' (Isaiah 46:10).

God does not need us or the rest of creation for anything. But everything depends on God. He requires no water, air, food, sleep, or money. The fortieth chapter of Isaiah makes these points by asking: "Have ye not known? Have ye not heard? Hath it not been told you from the foundations of the earth? It is God who sits upon the circle of the earth and we are like grasshoppers. He stretches out the heavens as a curtain and spreads them out as a tent to dwell in." (vv. 21-22). The Bible teaches that God determines the number of stars and He calls them by their names (Psalm 147:4). No one can do that but God. He is unequaled in all He is and does. He is the God that is beyond compare.

God is Invisible. There are numerous scripture references about the invisible God. Colossians 1:15 states, "He (Jesus) is the image of the invisible God, the firstborn of all creation." 1st Timothy 1:17 states, "Now to the King eternal, immortal, invisible, the only God, be honor and glory forever and ever. Amen." The invisibility of God is inseparably linked to our faith, our hope, and our love that is why it is impossible to please God without faith (Hebrews 11:6); we walk by faith and not by sight (2nd Corinthians 5:7); and the just shall live by faith (Habakkuk 2:4). Even the righteousness of God is revealed from faith to faith. We have to base our faith on the Word of God. It is God's Word that prompts us to look at the things that are not seen as written in 2nd Corinthians 4:18 *"So we fix our eyes not on what is seen, but on what is unseen, since what is seen is temporary, but what is unseen is eternal."*

The unseen plays a very significant part in the life of Believers, whose God is unseen by human eyes, but only seen with the eyes of faith. God is only visible to those who believe. Because God is invisible this is a major barrier that stands between the unbeliever and faith in God. The world says that seeing is believing, but this walk of faith says believing is seeing. In other words, seeing is and will never be sufficient basis for faith. Why? Because faith is rooted in a conviction concerning what is not seen as stated in Hebrews 11:1-2 "Now faith is being sure of what we hope for, being convinced of what we do not see. ² For by it the people of old received God's commendation." (NET)

It is God who opens the spiritual eyes of the unbeliever to be able to "see" Him who is unseen. Remember when Nicodemus encountered Jesus in the third chapter of John? Nicodemus was a Jewish ruler that came to Jesus at night. In the conversation, He said in verse 2, "Rabbi, we know that You have come from God as a teacher; for no one can do these signs that You do unless God is with him." Then Jesus replied, "Truly, truly, I say to you, unless one is born again, he cannot see the kingdom of God." Jesus' answered puzzled Nicodemus about being born again. I suggest you go and read the entire chapter. Nicodemus was a man whose life operated on the basis of what he saw. It was the custom and tradition of the Jews to be obsessed with externals and rituals and visible acts of righteousness. In Judaism, they did not put too much importance on matters of the heart or matters unseen and Jesus knew this about Nicodemus. "But Jesus said to them, "You are the ones who justify yourselves in men's eyes, but God knows your hearts. For what is highly prized among men is utterly detestable in God's sight." Luke 16:15 NET. It was more of religion than relationship.

However, with salvation, it is about what is unseen not seen. Salvation is not the result of man's striving and effort, but the result of God's invisible work. John 1:12-13 teaches, "But to all who have received him – those who believe in his name – he has given the right to become God's children– children not born by human parents or by human desire or a husband's decision, but by God." NET. God's salvation is the unseen work of the Holy Spirit that is accomplished in the heart. Jesus says this unseen work is the effects of the wind. No one sees the wind, but neither does anyone question where it exists. May God open our spiritual eyes to behold the wondrous things He has in store for His children. We are the Just and the Just shall live by faith not by sight (Habakkuk 2:4; 2 Corinthians 5:7; Romans 1:17; Hebrews

10:38).

God is Inscrutable. God's ways are perfect, but they are inscrutable (incomprehensible, beyond understanding) to you and me. In His essence, being, and existence, God is absolutely incomprehensible. His nature is immense and all of His holy properties are infinite. God is perfectly and completely known only to Himself. The Bible teaches that His thoughts are neither our thoughts, nor His ways ours for they are as the heavens (Isaiah 55:8-9). He is God and His ways are beyond our comprehension. He is the God that does everything well (Mark 7:37). Apostle Paul wrote in Romans 11:33-34, *"O the depth of the riches and the wisdom and knowledge of God! How inscrutable are his judgments! How unsearchable are his ways! For, 'Who has known the mind of the Lord? Who has been his counselor?'"* (CJB) What we know and what God knows are not even comparable. It is not that God is more intelligent than you and me, but His intelligence bears no resemblance to yours or mines. In other words, God's intelligence cannot be measured according to the same criteria as ours. Selah.

There is nobody like our God! Who is like our God? Isaiah 46:9 answers that question, "For I am God, and there is no other; I am God, and there is no one like Me." He is the God of Jeshurun Who rides the heavens to help us and through the skies in His majesty (Deuteronomy 33:26). He is the God that swears by His own self (Isaiah 45:23). Our God is completely unlike man. God is different and independent from His creation (Exodus 24:9-18; Isaiah 6:1-3; 40:12-26; 55:8-9). His being and existence are infinitely greater and higher than the His creation (1st Kings 8:27; Isaiah 66:1-2; Acts 17:24-25).

When God called Moses to lead the people of Israel, Moses wanted to know what to tell them who had sent him. In Exodus, Moses said to God, "If I come to the people of Israel and say to them, 'The God of your fathers has sent me to you,' and they ask me, 'What is his name?' what shall I say to them?" God said to Moses, **"I AM Who I AM."** And he said, "Say this to the people of Israel, "I AM has sent me to you." God also said to Moses, "Say this to the people of Israel, 'The

LORD, the God of your fathers, the God of Abraham, the God of Isaac, and the God of Jacob, has sent me to you'; this I my name for ever, and thus I am to be remembered throughout all generations." (Exodus 3:13-15). When God gave His name, (Ehyeh Asher Ehyeh) it is more accurately translated as I will be what I will be. God will be to us whoever and whatever He chooses to be – Father, Friend, Comforter, Counselor, or even disciplinarian. We can trust God's infinite wisdom to be who we need in our lives at each moment in time.

God is unchangeable/immutable. The God of the Universe has never evolved, grown, nor improved. Everything that His is today, He has ever been and will ever be. He is eternal. *"I the Lord do not change."* (Malachi 3:6). There was never a time that He did not exist and there will never come a time that He shall stop being God. God is unchangeable in His nature, His perfections, His purposes, His promises, His gifts and His holiness. God cannot turn to that which is evil. He is so glorious in His holiness; His deity cannot cease to be. God can NEVER change from righteousness to unrighteousness; from faithfulness to unfaithfulness; from holiness to unholiness. All things happen according to His unchangeable plans. God is perpetually the same. God must always deal with people according with His holy character and plan. God makes no deals or compromises and accepts no one apart from His plan of salvation in the person and work of Christ. Yet His unchangeable character is a constant comfort to us as believers because it means God is always faithful to His promises and the principles of His Word. God is "The Rock! His work is perfect, for all His ways are just; A God of faithfulness and without injustice, Righteous and upright is He. (Deuteronomy 32:4).

"Wherein God, willing more abundantly to shew unto the heirs of promise the immutability (unchangeable) of his council, confirmed it by an oath: That by two immutable things, in which it was impossible for God to lie, we might have a strong consolation, who have fled for refuge to lay hold unto the hope set before us (Hebrews 6:17-18)."

There is no one or nothing that can change God's plan. His

immutable purposes are always carried out. No angels or human have the power to stop the immutability of God. Psalm 33:11 states, "The council of the LORD standeth forever, the thoughts of his heart to all generations." Then again in Proverbs 21:30, "There is no wisdom nor understanding nor counsel against the LORD." Additionally, "There are many devices in a man's heart; nevertheless, the council of the LORD, that shall stand (Proverbs 19:21). Everything else changes but not God; He remains the same forever. (Psalm 119:89). Even His Word is irrevocable. Nor the wise or the evil can call it back (Isaiah 31:2).

We serve a God who will never cease to exist. He is not just eternal; He is absolutely unchangeable and unchanging. He is neither capable of nor susceptible to change. He can't change for the better or for the worse; He is already perfect! "As for God, his way is perfect: the word of the LORD is tried: he is a buckler to all those that trust him."

Because God is unchangeable, we can always trust and depend on Him. We can trust and depend on the love of God for it is everlasting (Jeremiah 31:3). We can trust and depend on His kindness (Isaiah 54:10). We can trust and depend on His Word. God's purpose is fixed, His will is stable, His word is sure (Isaiah 54:10).

God is omniscient / all-knowing. God knows all, past, present and future. He completely knows every detail about every life in heaven, earth, seas, and hell. There is nothing that escapes His knowledge. King David wrote in Psalm 139, "Thou knowest my downsitting and mine uprising, Thou understandest my thoughts afar off. Thou compassest my path and my lying down, and art acquainted with all my ways. For there is not a word in my tongue but, lo, O Lord, Thou knowest it altogether." (vv. 2-4). God possesses complete and universal knowledge, actual and possible. There is no limit to His knowledge. "Great is our Lord, and of great power: His understanding is infinite." (Psalm 147:5). God is not trying to learn anything new but knows everything at once. He knows the end from the beginning and everything in between. There is nothing hidden from Him. Hebrews

4:13 NIV teaches us, "Nothing in all creation is hidden from God's sight. Everything is uncovered and laid bare before the eyes of him to whom we must give account."

It is God who knows the name of the stars in sky. Just like He knows the names of each star, He also knows our name. He even knows the very hairs on our head. Matthew 10:30 states, "But even the hairs of your head are all numbered." God knew us before we were formed in the womb and had a plan for our lives before we were born. It is God who know us better than ourselves. He knows when we sit and when we rise. He perceives our thoughts from afar. David wrote in Psalm 139:1-4, "You have searched me, LORD, and you know me. You know when I sit and when I rise; you perceive my thoughts from afar. You discern my going out and my lying down; you are familiar with all my ways. Before a word is on my tongue, LORD, know it completely."

God already knew that His first humans would sin. Therefore, it is safe to say that when they sinned, Christ was already crucified in the mind of God. Revelation 13:8 tells us, "And all that dwell on the earth shall worship him, whose names are not written in the book of life of the Lamb slain from the foundation of the world." God knows that many will be saved through Christ's sacrifice and those who will be destroyed by His wrath. He knew those who would accept Christ and who would reject Him. In 2nd Timothy, it states, "Nevertheless the foundation of God standeth sure, having this seal, The Lord knoweth them that are his. And, let everyone that nameth the name of Christ depart from iniquity." (2:19). Our future is secure as born-again Believers because God knows.

So, God's knowledge does not come about from things because they were, are or will be but because He already knows it to be so. The infinite knowledge of God should fill us with amazement! It fills me with a holy awe! In fact, I become overwhelmed at thought of His omniscience. I delight in the Lord! Every born-again Believer should worship and adore our great God.

God is Omnipresent. When we talk about God being omnipresent, we're saying that He is capable of being everywhere at the same time. His divine presence encompasses the universe. Proverbs 15:3 teaches, "The eyes of the LORD are in every place, beholding the evil and the good." God is eternal and spatial dimensions cannot restrict Him. The highest heavens cannot contain Him (1st Kings 8:27). God is present to all space. That means that all space is presently before Him.

Though we cannot see His face, the omnipresence of God confirms that continually looks upon His creation. There is nothing hidden from Him. The whole earth is uncovered before Him. No matter where we go God is there (Psalm 139:7-12). In other words, God can be revealed both present to a person in a manifest manner (Psalm 46:1; Isaiah 57:15) and present in every situation in all of creation at any given time (Psalm 33:13-14). God can be present because He fills all things with His presence (Colossians 1:17) and He upholds everything by the Word of His Power (Hebrews 1:3).

Therefore, the omnipresence of God should remind us that we can never hide from God.

God is omnipotent. Plainly stated, God has all power over all things at all times and in all ways. Job said this about God's power: "I know that you can do all things and that no plan of yours can be thwarted." (Job 42:2). The power of God spoke, "Light Be" and it was so (Genesis 1:3). The whole world has been formed by the power of God's Word. I believe that the Book of Psalms gives special insights concerning God's omnipotence. For example, Psalm 33:6 states, "By the word of the LORD the heavens were made, and by the breath of his mouth all their host."

God's omnipotence is shown in all three Persons of the God head. In other words, God the Father, as stated in Job 42:2, can do all things. God the Son holds power over all nature and was involved in creation (John 1:2-3; Colossians 1:16-17). God the Holy Spirit was involved in creation and empowers believers (Genesis 1:2; Acts 2:41). In essence,

God's power gives us everything we need for life and godly living (2nd Peter 1:3). May each of us know the incomparably great power we have in God (Ephesians 1:19). Selah!

GOD IS LOVE
Chapter Four

John 3:16, *"For God so loved the world ..."* is a popular and familiar scripture that reminds us that God's love extends to the entire human race. He is no respecter of persons. He does not play favoritism. God's mercy extends to whom He will. "For he said Moses, I will have mercy on whom I will have mercy, and I will have compassion on whom I will have compassion (Romans 9:15).

It is not simply that God loves, but He is love itself. Love is His very nature. Sadly, there are many who talk about the love of God but misunderstand His love. This love does not mean that everything will be sweet, beautiful, and happy and that God's love could not possibly allow punishment for sin. After all, Jesus was punished for our sins and God loves Jesus and God loves us.

John 3:16 is a popular and familiar scripture that reminds us that God's love extends to the entire human race. He is no respecter of persons. He does not play favoritism.

In other words, when justice is preached, it is justice tempered with love. When righteousness of God is preached, it is righteousness founded in love. When atonement is preached, it is atonement planned by love, provided by love, given by love, finished by love, necessitated because of love. When the resurrection of Christ is preached, it is preaching the miracle of love. When the return of Christ is preached it is preaching the fulfillment of love. The love of God is AWESOME! God's love has no end, nor measure. No change can turn its course (Romans 8:35-39).

"God so loved the world that he gave his only begotten Son that whosoever believe on Him shall not perish but have everlasting life."

John 3:16

I believe this is one of the greatest verses in the Bible. His love is selfless love that embraces the whole world. By sending His only Son into the world is the greatest expression of this love towards sinful humanity. In this one verse we first see "God", the greatest person; "so loved" the greatest devotion; "the world", the greatest number; "he gave" the greatest act; "his only begotten Son" the greatest gift; "that whosoever believes" the greatest condition; "should not perish" the greatest mercy; "have everlasting life the greatest result." The initial work of God is for us to believe in Jesus Christ. John 6:29 teaches: "Jesus answered and said unto them, This is the work of God, that ye believe on him whom he hath sent." The revelation of God in the Bible reveals His infinite love and multifaceted grace. In God's love we enjoy His sustained favor.

He is the very epitome of what love in action really is. I believe love is at the very heart of who God is. We can see this is John 3:16. The love God has always sought the absolute and perfect well-being of the object loved (the world) regardless of the price or sacrifice (John 3:16; 1st John 3:16). Humanity's well-being is in the will of God, which is to bring man into conformity with His good and perfect will (Romans 12:1-2). In other words, God's love changes and transforms us to more like Him. We do that by living our life in Christ Jesus (2nd Thessalonians 3:5).

The Bible teaches that God is a jealous God (2nd Corinthians 11:2). Though God is a jealous God, His jealousy is not filled with possessiveness and suspicion as our jealousy. There isn't a hint of hatred, resentment or revenge in God. And God isn't insecure about who He is. God loves us with a perfect love, a love that casts out all fear and allows us to approach Him in complete freedom. 1st John 4:18 states, *"There is no fear in love; but perfect love casteth out fear."* God's love is perfect and we can trust His love. That very love is perfected in us when we love one another (1st John 4:12). The mutual abiding of the believer in God and God in the believer is manifested in love for others and this love produces a divine and human fellowship that testifies that we are disciples of Christ (John 13:34-35). As believers we can't even have faith without love because faith works by love (Galatians 5:6). This love can't be produced by our strength alone but it is the divine love that is shed abroad in our hearts by the Holy Spirit (Romans 5:5).

Moreover, the Bible teaches that if we love God, we will keep His commandments (John 14:15). These commandments are all of Jesus' words and teachings, which are God's Words. Jesus said, *"Anyone who loves me will obey my teaching. My Father will love them, and we will come to them and make our home with them. Anyone who does not love me will not obey my teaching. These words you hear are not my own; they belong to the Father who sent me."* (John 14:23-24). Only those who put faith in Jesus belongs to Him and are set free and obey His teachings or keep His commands (John 17:6). These "commands are not burdensome" (1st John 5:3). Why? Because we have been given the Holy Spirit to help us. Immediately after Jesus said to keep His commands, He said, "I will ask the Father, and he will give you another Counselor to be with you forever." (John 14:16). See, Jesus knows that we would need a divine source of power in order to keep His commands living in this sinful world. The Holy Spirit comes to live in us and brings with Him a totally different life of love, relationship, and service to the Lord.

Therefore, the love of God should cause us to love fellow believers as Jesus commanded in John 13:34. This love that comes flows from God through the Holy Spirit is a distinguishing mark of being a follower of Christ. It is a deep and sincere love for our brothers and sisters in Christ (1st John 4:21). Consequently, born-again believers are a people that the world has never seen before. In other words, Jesus did something that was very unique to the world and identified by one thing and that is L-O-V-E. Nothing else matters except the love we show towards one another. The God-love that is shown through believers is not like the love that is generated by the flesh. 1st Corinthians 13:4-8 shows us this supernatural love. I used to wonder how could I love a person like that. Then the Holy Spirit taught me how. He said that in order to love like this there must be a change of heart and begin to walk in the Spirit and be led by the Spirit (Galatians 5:16; Romans 8:14). It is possible to love like God because we have become partakers of the divine nature (2nd Peter 1:4).

God's love is a life of hope and truth in that He offers eternal life to humanity, in that the love of God was manifested toward to us that He sent His only Son into the world that we might have hope (life) through Him (1st John 4:9). Also, God's love aims at truth. In fact, truth serves love (1st Corinthians 13:6). We could say that love is happy when the truth of God is spoken in love (Ephesians 4:16). The reality is this, God's love is life changing. For the Christian, it is the very foundation of how we should live our life in Christ.

GOD'S LOVE IS A-W-E-S-O-M-E!

Available
With us
Everlasting
Selfless
Obtainable
Mesmerizing (compelling)
Easy

THE TRINITY: GOD FATHER, GOD SON, GOD HOLY SPIRIT
Chapter Five

There is only one God, but in the unity of the Godhead there are three eternal and coequal Persons equal in attributes. The Trinity is God the Father, above us; God the Son, beside us; and God the Spirit, within us. God is more loving, nurturing and compassionate than the most loving, nurturing and compassionate mother. God the Son, the God-man, is more noble, courageous and purposeful than the most noble, courageous, and purposeful of men. God the Holy Spirit is more powerful, truthful, wiser, intelligent than the most powerful, most truthful, the wisest of the most intelligent of humans. God the Trinity is truly an awesome wonder to our soul.

In Genesis, the first book of the Bible, chapter one, we see the three Persons appear. The Spirit hovering over the great deep and right in the midst of the text, God the Father and God the Son speak to each other about the creation of humanity. The first use of the trinity is chapter one and verse 1: In the beginning, Elohim created the heaven and the earth. Right from the start, this plural form for the name of God is used to describe the One God, a mystery that is uncovered throughout the rest of the Bible.

Now although the Divine Persons are in the Old Testament, the names are not as distinct as in the New Testament. For instance, in the Old Testament the Holy Spirit does divine things, the Angel of the Lord will be called God the Son, and God the Father will be the God of the Highest Heaven. It is not until the New Testament that they are more distinctive in terms of individuals, but still the Oneness of Deity. The true and living God is vastly superior to other gods of this world. Exodus 15:11 states, *"Who is like unto thee, O LORD, among the gods? Who is like thee, glorious in holiness, fearful in praises, doing wonders?"*

God is a trinity. In Matthew 3:16-17, we see the Godhead in the baptism of Christ. "And Jesus, when he was baptized, went up straight way out of the water and, lo, the heavens were opened unto him, and he saw the Spirit of God descending upon him: And lo a voice from heaven, saying, This is my beloved Son, in whom I am well pleased." Then in John 14:16, we see the Godhead in the teaching of Jesus. "And I will pray the Father, and he shall give you another Comforter, that he may abide with you forever." We also see the Trinity in the Great Commission. Matthew 28:19 states, *"Go ye therefore, and teach all nations, baptizing them in the name of the Father, and of the Son, and of the Holy Ghost."* Even in apostolic benediction 2nd Corinthians 13:14 shows the Godhead. *"The grace of the Lord Jesus Christ, and the love of God, and the communion of the Holy Ghost, be with you all. Amen."* Though the Trinity is a mystery to some, it is not to those who believe this by faith. Hebrew 11:6 tells us, *"But without faith it is impossible to please him; for he that cometh to God must believe that he is, and that he is a rewarder of them that diligently seek him."*

God, Father, Son, and Holy Ghost are coequal Persons. They have the same exact attributes but with different functions. Though they are equal they are not the same. In other words, the Father is not the Son or the Holy Spirit. The Son is not the Father or the Holy Spirit. The Holy Spirit is not the Father or the Son. Yet, each Person of the Trinity is God. The function of the God the Father is the ultimate source or cause of the universe (1st Corinthians 8:6, Revelation 4:11); divine revelation (John 1:1, 16:12-15; Matthew 11:27; Revelation 1:1); salvation (2nd Corinthians 5:19, Matthew 1:21, John 4:42); and Jesus' human works (John 5:17; 14:10). It is the God the Father who initiates all of these things. He is the One who does the drawing (John 6:44).

The function or work of the God the Son is being the agent through whom the Father does the following works: the creation and maintenance of the universe (1st Corinthians 8:6; John 1:3; Colossians 1:16-17); divine revelation (John 1:1, 16:12-15; Matthew 11:27; Revelation 1:1); and salvation (2nd Corinthians 5:19; Matthew 1:21; John

4:42). It is God the Father that does all these things through the Son, who functions as His agent. Now God the Holy Spirit is the means by whom the Father does the following works: creation and maintenance of the universe (Genesis 1:2; Job 26:13; Psalm 104:30); divine revelation and illumination (John 6:12-15; Ephesians 3:5; 2 Peter 1:21); salvation (John 3:6; Titus 3:5; 1st Peter 1:2); and Jesus' works (Isaiah 61:1; Acts 10:38). So, it is God the Father who does all these things by the power of the Holy Spirit. In Essence, the Holy Spirit was sent to reveal the Son and the Son was sent to reveal the Father.

"O righteous Father, the world hath not known thee: but I have known thee, and these have known that thou hast sent me. And I have declared unto them thy name and will declare it: that the love where with thou hast loved me may be in them, and I in them." **John 17:25-26.**

I have heard several illustrations of the Trinity. One of the most popular is the forms of water. I really don't believe these illustrations give justice to describing the Trinity. See the Father, Son, and Holy Spirit is not parts of God because each of them is God. The same way they are not forms of God, because they are God.

GOD THE FATHER: GOD ABOVE
Chapter Six

One God and Father of all, who is over all and through all and in all. Ephesian 4:6

When God is spoken of as the Father of all men, it is as Creator (Malachi 2:10). It is in the general sense to everyone because all people are created by God in His image. Hebrews 12:9 tells us that God is the Father of spirits (Numbers 16:22, Ecclesiastes 12:7). We are all offspring of God as stated in Acts 17:28. However, it does not mean that everyone will have eternal life. God is as the Father who is the sustainer of all life and each person is the object of God's fatherly care (Matthew 18:10) and a candidate for His Kingdom (Luke 18:16). In the Bible, the word "Father" is used in a variety of ways. For instance, as the Father of Jesus, it is used as an eternal, unique relationship; as the Father of Believers, it represents a relationship established by grace; and as Father of Israel, it means a bond established by covenant.

For a sinner to become a child of God, a miraculous transformation has to take place. The sinner has to be "born again" (John 3:3) by placing his faith in Christ as Savior. It is then he is born again into a new spiritual family relationship with God as Father (Hebrews 3:1). Not only is he a child of God by spiritual birth but also adopted as well (Galatians 4:1-5). This divine relationship carries responsibilities with it, as well as privileges. Therefore, he /she bears the family relationship to God, he / she must also exhibit the family character.

God the Father has lavished His great love on us and now we are called children of God! (1ˢᵗ John 3:1). Anytime we are asked the question: Who are you? We should not hesitate to answer: *"I am a child of the Most High God!"* It is worthy to note that God did not become a Father when we were saved, but His fatherhood is eternal. Remember God has always been God. He has always existed. His very name is Yahweh which means "I Am" because He always has been and always will be.

It is through Jesus we receive the Father's love and are called "children of God." John 1:12 tells us that God gives us the right to become children of God to all who in faith have received Christ as Lord and Savior. It is the most marvelous thing to know that as God for our Father, we enjoy all rights and privileges our adoption entails. We are heirs of God and joint heirs with Christ (Romans 8:17). Therefore, we put our trust and faith in Him to provide for us and to protect us.

God as Father is the Supreme Being, Creator and Sustainer. He deserves our worship and obedience. He can only be known by faith in Jesus Christ. Jesus said that He did what He saw His Father do and say what He hears His Father says (John 5:19).

GOD THE SON: GOD BESIDE
Chapter Seven

"O righteous Father, the world hath not known thee: but I have known thee, and these have known that thou hast sent me. And I have declared unto them thy name and will declare it: that the love where with thou hast loved me may be in them, and I in them." **John 17:25-26**

I believe that our relationship with the Son determines whether we will become Christians. Jesus is the hero of the whole Bible. He is the Savior of the world. He delivers us from the penalty of sin (Justification), the power of sin (sanctification) and ultimately the presence of sin (Glorification). A Biblical understanding of Jesus Christ is crucial to our salvation. Why? Because Jesus is the atoning sacrifice for our sins. He had to become man so He could die and at the same time He had to be God so that His death would pay for our sins. He had to be the sacrifice as well as the One who gave the sacrifice (John 15:13). He was fully man and fully God.

Christ is our High Priest and our Sacrifice. The Bible says He is a Priest in the order of Melchizedek, which means King of Righteousness. God sent a new and different rank of priest in Jesus Christ. He was from a different tribe and no one from that tribe ever officiated at God's altar. Essentially, Jesus did not descend from the tribe of Levi but the tribe of Judah. Jesus as our King-Priest was not made after the law of legal requirement but after the power of an indestructible, resurrection life. (Hebrews 7:12-16). Jesus was made our guarantee of a better agreement than what was before. Jesus our Savior, Lord, and King permanently and completely holds His priestly office because He lives forever and will NEVER have a successor. That is the

Good News for us. Why? Because Jesus is able to save fully everyone who comes to God through Him. Jesus is our High Priest who lives to pray without ceasing for us. He is the High Priest who perfectly fits our need – holy, without a trace of evil, without the ability to deceive, incapable of sin, and exalted beyond the heavens! (Hebrews 7:25-26).

Jesus offered a perfect sacrifice in heaven. He serves in the holy sanctuary in the true heavenly tabernacles set up by God and not by men. Hebrews 8:1 state, *"Now of the things which we have spoken this is the sum: We have such an high priest, who is set on the right hand of the throne of the Majesty in the heavens." (KJV)* In other words, our King-Priest ministers at the right of hand of God and He is enthroned with honor next to the throne of the Majesty on High. Selah.

Through Christ sacrifice, He became the mediator of a better covenant established on better promises (Hebrews 8:6). The better covenant is the New Covenant and is the basis of Ministry. Jesus Christ has made us communicators of this New Covenant of the spirit that gives life. In other words, we are epistles of Christ written with the Spirit of the living God in our hearts (2nd Corinthians 3:3-6).

Through Jesus, rejected by humans but chosen by God, the Living Stone, we also are like living stones who are being built into a spiritual house to be a holy priesthood. As a holy priesthood, we are to offer spiritual sacrifices acceptable to God through Jesus Christ. (1st Peter 2:4-6). We are admonished by Apostle Paul to present our bodies a living sacrifice, holy, acceptable unto God, which is our reasonable service (Romans 12:1). Our body is the temple of the Holy Spirit (1st Corinthians 3:16-17).

What a wonderful Covenant we have in Christ and through Christ. It is a perfect covenant. Christ has become High Priest and King of wonderful things to come by a greater and more perfect tabernacle not made by people. He has secured our eternity because He has entered once and forever into the Holiest Sanctuary of all by the sacred blood of His own sacrifice. It is He who has made our salvation secure forever! (Hebrews 9:11-12). We now can have a new relationship with God and we receive the eternal inheritance He has promised to His children (Hebrews 9:15). We are heirs of God and joint heirs with Jesus Christ (Romans 8:17). Because of the Blood of Jesus, we have confidence before God.

"Having therefore, brethren, boldness (opportunity) to enter into the holiest by the blood of Jesus, By a new and living way, which he hath consecrated (prepared) for us, through the veil, that is to say, his flesh; And having an (a great) high priest over (in charge) the house of God; Let us draw near with a true heart in full assurance of faith, having our hearts sprinkled from an evil conscience, and our bodies washed with pure water. Let us hold (be persistent) the profession of our faith without wavering; (for he is faithful that promised;)." *Hebrews 10:19:23 KJV*

Scriptures describes humility as meekness, lowliness, and absence of self. Colossians 3:12 states, *"Put on then, as God's chosen ones, holy and beloved, compassionate hearts, kindness, humility, meekness, and patience."* Humility is a heart attitude, not just an outward show. Some may put on an outward show like they are humble but their heart is full of pride and arrogance. Jesus teaches about humility in Matthew 5:3. He said that those who are "poor in spirit" would have the kingdom of heaven. In other words, being poor in spirit means that only those who admit to an absolute bankruptcy of spiritual worth will inherit life. Christians must have humility in order to come Jesus.

Apostle Paul give revelation of the humility of Jesus Christ in Philippians 2:5-16. Christ humbled Himself when He left His home in Glory to become a servant of man. He even took on a human name as part of that humility. Philippians 2:7 teaches that Jesus "emptied Himself, taking the form of a bond-servant, and being made in the likeness of men." This is known as "kenosis", a Greek word that means self-renunciation. It wasn't that He was emptying Himself of His deity nor was it Him exchanging His deity for humanity. Jesus did not stop being God but He was human. He was fully God and fully human. But

He was completely submitted to the will of the Father in obedience and humility. He was subject to human limitations. John 4:6 states, "Jacob's well was there; so Jesus, wearied as he was from his journey, was sitting beside the well. It was about the sixth hour (ESV). Even on the Cross His human side was present. He said, *"I Thirst."* (John 19:28 ESV). In His great humility, He added the human nature. He went from being the Word in Eternity to being made flesh who was crucified on the Cross.

"But made himself of no reputation, and took upon him the form of a servant, and was made in the likeness of men: And being found in fashion as a man, he humbled himself, and became obedient unto death, even the death of the cross." Philippians 2:7-8

Jesus died a criminal's death and was not a criminal. He did as us and for us. And with the example that He gives us to be humble, we must come to Him in humility. We have to acknowledge that we are destitute, poor, miserable, a wretch, etc. who is before him with nothing to offer Him but our sin and our need for salvation. Then through grace by faith we accept the precious gift of the salvation of our soul. We commit our life to Him and to others. In other words, we die to self so that we now live as new creations in Christ. *"Therefore, if any man is in Christ, he is a new creation. The old has passed away; behold, the new has come."* (2nd Corinthians 5:17). We now began to walk in the exchange we were given by way of the Cross and His Resurrection. Because He exchanged our worthlessness for His infinite worth, our sin for His righteousness, and the life we now live, we live by faith in the Son of God who loved us and gave Himself for us.

"I am crucified with Christ: nevertheless I live; yet not I, but Christ liveth in me: and the life which I now live in the flesh I live by faith of the Son of God, who loved me, and gave himself for me." – Galatians 2:20

Jesus exhibited true humility. And because of that God exalted Him and multiplied His greatness. Jesus now has the greatest name in heaven and on earth. His name has been given all authority and power for everyone will reverence Him!

"Wherefore God also hath highly exalted him, and given him a name that is above every name. That at the name of Jesus every knew should bow, of things under the earth: And that every tongue should confess that Jesus Christ is Lord, to the glory of God the Father." – Philippians 2:9-10

Jesus Christ said He did not come to be serve but to serve. He was not ashamed to humble Himself to be a servant. Mark 10:45 states, "For even the Son of Man did not come to be served, but to serve, and to give his life as a ransom for many. (NIV). As He did in servanthood, so should commit ourselves to serving others. This humility is not only necessary to enter the Kingdom but it is also necessary to be great in the Kingdom. *"It shall not be so among you. But whoever would be great among you must be your servant, and whoever would be first among you must be your slave."* (Matthew 20:26-27 ESV). Genuine humility produces godliness, contentment and security. As we humble ourselves, we are given more grace and is exalted (Luke 14:11).

GOD THE HOLY SPIRIT: GOD WITHIN
Chapter Eight

*Do you not know that you are the sanctuary of God and
that the Spirit of God dwells in you?*
1st Corinthians 3:16

When a person is born again, the Holy Spirit takes up residence in their heart. He was given after Jesus ascended back to the Father. We have to first understand that the Holy Spirit is a Person. He has the same divine nature as the Father and the Son. He is not some mysterious influence that somehow, we have to get hold of or try to catch. He is a real person, infinitely holy, infinitely wise, infinitely mighty and infinitely powerful who is to get hold of us and use us. It is often said that we got the Holy Spirit but it should be that the Holy Spirit has us. In other words, it's not that we get more of the Spirit but He gets more of us.

The Holy Spirit the power; the anointing of God. He is the connection to the Father and the Son. The Holy Spirit helps us to know a living God who acts and speaks today, a God who is ready to come as near to us as He came to Abraham, Moses, Isaiah, Elijah and the Apostles. Just like with Jesus, we can be clothed with the Holy Spirit. The Bible teaches that when Jesus was baptized, the Holy Spirit came upon Him in the form of a dove and remained on Him (Matthew 3:16; Mark 1:10; Luke 3:22; John 1:32). When Jesus came out of the wilderness, He stood up and declared that He was anointed for the assignment God gave Him (Luke 4:18). So, with Believers Jesus Christ has given the Holy Spirit for what we have been called to do.

Christ gives the Holy Spirit to live in a way that pleases God (Gal.

5:16-25). The Holy Spirit empowers Born-again believers to live and work with Christlikeness. Spirituality has to do with character and conduct, regardless of where we are. Remember that scripture teaches that we are the sanctuary of the Holy Spirit (1st Corinthians 6:19). With the power of the Holy Ghost we can expect Him to enable us to use our God-given skills and abilities to bring glory to God. When we open and be ourselves, the Holy Spirit can orchestrate our lives to others and make us pleasing to God. Our relationship with the Spirit of God determines what kind of Believers we will become. The Holy Spirit has to apply biblical truth to the heart of the people. Afterall, we must be ambassadors through whom He can introduce Jesus. Because there is a world out there hungry and searching for Jesus and His love.

The Holy Spirit is ready to come and take His place in our heart. We just need to surrender to Him and ask to be filled by His power. When I say filled, I am talking about being controlled by Him in every area of our life. It is to allow Him to bring everything in thought, feelings, actions, purpose and imagination into conformity with His will. We can do this because we recognize His Presence, His gracious and glorious indwelling and give Him complete control.

The indwelling Spirit is a source of full and everlasting satisfaction and successful Christian living. The Holy Spirit completely and forever satisfies the person who allows Him to be in control. We have to realize that we are helpless in living an effective and successful life as a Christian without Him. If we were to take our eyes off of Jesus Christ, if we were to neglect the study of the Word and prayer, it would be very harmful to our Christian walk. We MUST continuously live in the Spirit and walk in the Spirit if we would have a victorious Christian life (Galatians 5:16, 25).

I can remember going to church Sunday after Sunday and leaving the same way I came; leaving not knowing how to deal with the challenges I was facing. As these challenges became greater and greater, even to the point of torment, it was at that point I needed help. I was baptized in the name of the Father, the Son, and the Holy Spirit. I didn't know that was in the Bible. No amount of preaching or singing was helping me.

As my life sank deeper in the despair of the pit of depression and hopelessness, I knew I had to do something. The Lord heard my heart's cry even when I didn't know what to pray or how to pray. My tears became my prayers. My sister, Louise, invited me to a class at her church on the Holy Spirit. I went through that class seeking the Holy Spirit for help, but after the class ended nothing had changed for me. It wasn't until I turned to God and cried out in desperation for help; I had gotten to the end of myself. I gave up struggling and striving in my own strength and I looked up to the Lord and honestly and humbly confessed that I was down as low as I have ever been and if He didn't pick me up, I would never get up. The next thing I knew, I was instantly on my feet and a peace came over me like I never experienced.

Before long, I was able to open my Bible and understand what I was reading. Then I was led to the Gospel according to John. I became so hungry for the Truth of God! The next stop was the Book of Acts to show me the Holy Spirit. I knew then that the Holy Spirit was missing from me being able to deal with my problems. The more He poured into me the more I decreased. I took my mind off of me and pursued God's Word like never before. I do believe Matthew 6:33, *"Seek ye first the Kingdom of God and His righteousness and all others will be added unto thee."* Then He took me to the Book of Romans. Oh my! I just began to transform more and more. With every Word my eyes devoured, the Holy Spirit quickened it and my heart closed around it by faith. There was such a harvest in my life from my encounter with the Holy Spirit at the lowest point in my life. The Holy Spirit is not just a guest to me but He is the owner of the "house."

My experience with the Holy Spirit is very sweet and tender. I can remember when the Father was drawing me into a relationship with Christ, the Holy Spirit was right there guiding me every step of the way. I knew I had gotten to a place where I needed more than I was getting on Sunday mornings. I became so desperate for more. I began to pursue the Word of God. I learned of the Holy Spirit in John. Then I saw that I could speak with the language of the Holy Spirit and I wanted this experience. I asked and was given a language I did not know and I did not study. No one taught it to me. From that moment, the Holy Spirit became my friend. He taught me a strong foundation in Christ Jesus. He became my revelation-Light into the heart and mind of God. Oh, I cannot do without Him. I heard the late Katherine Kuhlman say in one of her messages that we are not to grieve the Holy Spirit because He is all she has. Something stirred deep within me as I heard that and I have made it a priority to always talk to Holy Spirit on an intimate and personal level. I know I need Him, always. The best thing any True Believer can do is make friends with the Holy Spirit. Be determined to partner with Him.

He has taught me every step of the way. I can relate to Paul when he said that he did not "consult with flesh and blood" (Galatians 1:16). For twelve years, I was the private student to the Holy Spirit. I hungered and thirsted for righteousness and I was fed. He built such a foundation for me in the Word of God. How wonderful that was for me and still is. I know from my own experience that I started off at ground level with my knowledge of the Bible. His conversation is so sweet and wholesome and enriching. Everything about Him is so wholesome and delightful, yet He is so powerful. Reading John 16:13, I knew I had to have the Spirit of Truth in my life because I needed truth. I needed the Teacher of Truth more than anything. When I was introduced to Acts 1:8, I had to have what Jesus told His disciples to wait for to be a witness unto Him.

Listen, I was so glad when I came to know the Holy Spirit as the Paraclete. When I thought about How He stands beside me and He stands in me. When I stand up to speak before a group of people, I know I can count on Him to do the work. I try to stand back as far as possible for Him to do the work. Not only then but He is there when I am in prayer (Romans 8:26-27). He is there when I read my Bible (John 14:26; 16:12-14). He is there when I am on my job (Acts 8:29). He is there when I am tempted (Romans 8:2). Even when I leave this world, He is with me (Acts 7:54-60). Oh, I need Holy Spirit! I say with King David in Psalm 51:11, "Do not cast me from your presence or take your Holy Spirit from me."

I can remember in 2015 (December 16th) I prayed this prayer:

Heavenly, Father just as I thank You for Your Son, Jesus Christ, I also thank You for the Presence of the Holy Spirit.

As I get to know Him more and more, He gets more of me, and as He gets more of me, You get more of me.

I am so grateful for His coming after Jesus went back to Your side. I thank Jesus that He did not leave us comfortless, but He sent another Comforter who is just as Divine as He is, just as loving as He is, just as tender as He is, just as ready and able to help and is always by our side and we are His sanctuary. All we have to do is to trust Him as we trust You and the Son.

I trust Him by Your grace to be my Comforter, my Teacher, my Truth, my Light, my Guide, my Protection, my Healer, my Mouthpiece giving me the words to say, my Revealer and Illuminator in the deep things of God. I do recognize His Presence, His gracious and glorious indwelling. So, help me Father not to ever grieve or quench the Holy Spirit. I give Him complete control of this house He already has residence in.

I just want to say thank You, God, Father, Son, and Holy Ghost. You are my life. Amen!

I pray for every Believer that Christ be formed in you by the Holy Spirit as Apostle Paul prayed in Ephesians 3:16-19:

"I pray that out of his glorious riches he may strengthen you with power through his Spirit in your inner being, so that Christ may dwell in your hearts through faith. And I pray that you, being rooted and established in love, may have power, together with all the Lord's holy people, to grasp how wide and long and high and deep is the love of

Christ, and to know this love that surpasses knowledge – that you may be filled to the measure of all the fullness of God." Amen!

All this can be stated simply and plainly as this: The Father has chosen us for salvation, loves us, and gives us consolation and hope (2nd Thessalonians 2:13). The Son shares His glory with each of us and provides comfort and a sure foundation in the faith (2nd Thessalonians 2:14, 16). The Spirit purifies, transforms and matures our faith. (2nd Thessalonians 2:13).

KNOWING GOD
Chapter Nine

We will come to know more and more about God as we obey Him. Thusly, our knowledge and understanding of God should be greater now than when we first became born-again. Yet, sadly, some continue to live year after year with the same basic knowledge of God that they had when they first began walking with Him. Apostle Paul calls these believers infants and carnal minded and not able to understand spiritual teaching (1ˢᵗ Corinthians 3:1-4). We get to know God by simply spending time with Him.

Deuteronomy 29:29 teaches us, "The secret things belong to the Lord our God; but the things revealed belong to us and to our children forever, that we may practice all the words of this law." This means, in essence, that there is an area of knowledge that God has kept secret from us. Yet there is an area of knowledge that He has revealed to us in Scripture. What belongs to God belongs to God and what knowledge has been given to us must be known and taught to all generations. However, this knowledge that we may practice all the words of this law. In other words, Scripture consist of revealed truths which are capable of application to life. Bible principles must be put into practice.

Therefore, God has made it so that we can personally know Him. God is knowable and we can grow in the knowledge of God to the degree we need to trust Him and have a personal and growing relationship with Him. The Bible gives us clear principles explaining how we can begin a relationship with God through Jesus Christ. Jesus answered, *"I am the way and the truth and the life. No one comes to the Father except through me."* (John 14:6) Therefore, each person must receive Jesus Christ as Savior and Lord; then we can know and experience God's love and purpose for our lives. We must turn to God in repentance and have faith in our Lord Jesus (Acts 20:21).

We can know God through a personal relationship with Him because of the death and resurrection of Christ that removed the barrier of the sin that separated us from Him (Galatians 4:3-9; Hebrews 8:11-12). Once we have put faith in the work of God's Son and received salvation, there is much more of God to experience. Our conversion is just the beginning of a lifelong spiritual journey in knowing God. This kind of knowing God goes hand in hand with living a godly lifestyle. If we claim to know God, then the way we live our lives should prove it (James 2:17; 1st John 1:6; 4:7). Having a personal relationship with God, based on faith in Jesus Christ, is crucial and essential as a believer and witness of Him.

We serve the One and Only True God and knowing Him is eternal life. John 17:3 teaches: "Now this is eternal life: that they know you, the only true God, and Jesus Christ, whom you have sent." (NIV) God is REAL "...For since the creation of the world God's invisible qualities – His eternal power and divine nature – have been clearly seen, being understood from what has been made, so that people are without excuse." (Romans 1:19-20). There are those who try to suppress the knowledge of God, and some try to add to it. But as Christians, we have should have a deep desire to know God; His work and His ways. "Show me how you work, God; School me in your ways." (Psalm 25:4)

The first step to take in knowing God is faith. We must first know Jesus Christ, who was sent from God (John 6:38). When we are born-again by the power of the Holy Spirit, we can begin to learn about God, His character, and His will. Knowing God takes the Spirit of God for it is the Spirit that searches all things, even the deep things of God (1st Corinthians 2:10). Having a personal and intimate relationship with God based on faith in Jesus is essential. And that relationship has to be reflected in what we do. We must be careful about claiming to know God but act as if we have never heard of Him (Luke 6:46-49). And it starts with a healthy relationship of the knowledge of who God is which should mature into a deeper personal experience of how we live our life.

Jesus the Messiah was sent to be both the revelation of God to man and the reconciliation of man to God prayed this in John 17:3, *"And this is eternal life, that they may know Thee, the Only True God, and Jesus Christ whom Thou hast sent."* Christ Himself declared that knowing God is the essence of eternal life. He wasn't just saying that this is the way to getting into heaven, but it was of knowing and experiencing an eternal quality of life now, a life of meaning, purpose, and usefulness to God and humanity with peace and joy. I believe that all life's issues and questions ultimately find their answers in the knowledge of God that comes through Jesus Christ.

The Bible is the primary source to gain accurate knowledge of God. In the Scriptures we find that God is Spirit. He is a living and active divine person who is infinite, eternal, and unchangeable in His being, wisdom, power, holiness, justice, goodness, truth, and love. God is so overwhelmingly amazing. He pervades and sustains the universe, yet He is always distinct from it. He is everywhere, yet not in everything. He is personally and intimately involved yet distinct (Proverbs 5:21; Psalms 33:13-14; Romans 11:34-36).

Remember God wants us to know Him. He desires that we love Him. "And you shall love the LORD your God with all your heart, with all your soul, with all your mind, and with all your strength. (Mark 12:30 NKJV). This is the first commandment. I believe the more we come to know God and His goodness, the more we come to know love. Why? Because God is love. As more of His everlasting love for us is revealed, the more we will love Him. We love Him because He first loved us. (1st John 4:19 NKJV)

Additionally, in order to avoid being deceived, we must learn who God is and what God is like from His God-breathed revelation to us in the Bible. This is an essential goal and foundational truth to our intimate walk with God. The facts are foundational truths and the goal is fellowship with God. As we continue to learn of Him, we also learn about His person, plan, purposes, principles, and promises. Our revelation of God is what builds our faith, gives us peace, comfort, courage, joy, and the grace to deal with the everyday life. It is not just the knowledge about God, but the knowledge of God that is absolutely critical to our ability to live the godly life we have been called to live. Selah.

Thus, as God reveals His character to us in the Bible and by His Spirit, we know more of Him, and the more we know of Him personally, the more the love we have for Him will grow. And a person who loves God will obey Him.

So, my question to you is this: Does your lifestyle reflect your relationship with God? Be very careful of claiming that you know God but act if you have never met Him or heard about Him (Luke 6:46-49).

THE WORD OF GOD
Chapter Ten

"Forever, O LORD, thy word is settled in heaven."
Psalm 119:89

*"All Scripture is God breathed and is useful for teaching,
rebuking, correcting and training in righteousness."*
2 Timothy 3:16

The Bible is the Word of God. It is the greatest book ever written. I call it the "Manufacture's Manual" because it is a book of divine instruction from the Creator to the created. Though His word is eternal and stands firm in the heavens (Psalm 119:89; Isaiah 40:8; 1st Peter 1:24-25) it is not a static word. It is living and active and powerful (Hebrews 4:12). In this one book alone, there is comfort in sorrow, guidance in perplexity, advice for our problems, rebuke for our sins, and daily inspiration for our every need. It's not just simply one book but it is an entire library of books. In other words, it includes history, poetry, drama, biography, prophecy, philosophy, science, and inspirational reading.

The Bible reveals the truth about God, explains the human origin, points out the only way to salvation and eternal life, and explains the age-old problem of sin and suffering. Jesus Christ and His work of redemption for mankind is the central theme of the Bible. In this great Book, the Person and work of Jesus Christ are promised, prophesied, and pictured in the types, symbols, and shadows of the Old Testament. In the New Testament, His truth and beauty are revealed in the Gospels. In the Epistles, the full meanings of His life, His death, and His resurrection are explained. The in the Book of Revelation His glorious coming again to earth in the future is unmistakably foretold. The great purpose of the Bible is to reveal the living Word of God, Jesus Christ, Lord, Savior, and King (John 1:1-18).

The Bible is a book of faith. Therefore, we have to believe what is written in it by faith. I started studying the Bible because I needed help that went beyond human ability or knowledge. Once I started reading and studying the Word of God, I have not put it down. Over 19 years I have be growing in the grace and knowledge of Jesus Christ. Maturing in knowledge is very important to me because it builds my relationship with God, along with prayer and the Holy Spirit. God has given us the Bible in order that we might know Him and that we might do His will here on earth. There is an old adage that states, "Sin will keep you from God's Word, and God's Word will keep you from sin."

The Bible is the Christian's guide to the new life in knowing God's Word, understanding God's Being, beginning the new life, growing in the new life, facing problems in the new life and recognizing God's institutions. We can realize our place in God's program and work to fulfill our destines. This is why it is extremely important to grow in this new life, "to desire the pure milk of the word" (1st Peter 2:2). Through the Holy Spirit, prayer, and worship, if we submit to the lordship of Jesus in reverence and service, we will grow in our spiritual life. Growing in the Word produces growth in faith. And reading and understanding the Word are like planting seeds of faith in our heart that will bear the mature fruit of faith.

Therefore, we must be careful not to just read the Bible informationally but also relationally. When we approach the Bible informationally, it is to elevate our knowledge, but when we approach the Bible relationally, we elevate our affection and love for God. The more I learn about God, the more I love Him. Remember this Book is not just a book with great truth and accurate information. Behind this Book is a personal God who desires a personal relationship with each of us. This has always been God's plan from the beginning of time when He created man in His image and likeness. Though the fellowship and communion were broken by Adam and Eve, we have the redemption that Jesus brings to reconcile us back to the Father. So, once we understand God desires a relationship with us, we should more than ever recognize we truly need Him. Apostle Paul put it this way in 2nd Corinthians 3:5 (REB), *"There is no question of our having sufficient power in ourselves: we cannot claim anything as our own. The power we have comes from God."* It is God who loved us first that we may also love Him. What a magnificent love God has bestowed on us that we are called children of God (1st John 3:1-3).

God's Word is what we need for the new life. It teaches us what is true and make us realize what is wrong in our lives. It corrects us when we are wrong and teaches us to do what is right. There are no excuses. We have been given the Holy Word of God so that we may be complete, fully equipped for every good work (2nd Timothy 3:16). God's word is alive and powerful because God is at work in and through it (Hebrews 4:12). The Word is Spirit and when we apply it to our life we are sanctified and built up in our faith. Jesus tells us in John 17:16-19 that we have a practical progressive sanctification of our new life by the application of the truth of the Word of God. The Word of God has the liberty in the heart of the Spirit-led Believer to displace sin and replace in its place the righteousness of God. Therefore, it is our responsibility to apply the Word of God each day by the power of the Holy Spirit.

The most important thing about God's Word is not just that it is to read and studied, but that we live it, that we obey the Lord (James 1:22) God did not give us His Word to just inform us, but to change us and transform us. Remember, The Bible is ALWAYS relevant to our lives because God is ALWAYS relevant to our lives. Like 2nd Timothy 3:16 teaches, it is profitable for doctrine for the teaching of the great truth of God Himself. It is profitable for reproof in convicting us of the unrighteousness in our life. It is profitable for correction when we are in error to show us the right way. Then it is profitable for instruction in righteousness to allow Born again Believers to become fully equipped for every good work. The people of God have to read it (Revelation 1:3; Colossians 3:16), Heed it (1st Timothy 4:16), and feed it (Matthew 28:19-20). I read somewhere that the child of God is to know the Word of God, store it in their heart, apply it in their life, and teach it.

Simply put, the authoritative Bible, the Word of God:

- Upholds how we live (**Psalm 119:116**)
- Orders and directs our steps (**Psalm 119:133**)
- Produces joy and riches (**Psalm 119:162**)
- Gives strength (**Psalm 119:74**)
- Gives light (**Psalm 119:105**)
- Gives hope (**Psalm 119:74**)
- Gives understanding (**Psalm 119:169**)
- Accomplish the plans of God (**Isaiah 55:11**)
- Is able to build up (**Acts 20:32**)
- Produces results (**John 15:7**)
- Is a discerner of the thoughts and intents of the heart (**Hebrews 4:12**)
- Causes conversion of the soul (**James 1:18; Romans 10:17**)
- Cleanses and corrects (**John 15:3; Psalm 119:9**)
- Sanctifies (**John 17:17**)
- Comforts and make alive (**Psalm 119:50**)

Therefore, God charges those who teach the word to handle it correctly and to preach it faithfully (1ˢᵗ Timothy 5:17; 2ⁿᵈ Timothy 2:15; 2ⁿᵈ Timothy 4:2). Additionally, ALL believers are called to proclaim the Word of God wherever they go (Acts 8:4).

GOD IN THE PSALMS
Chapter Eleven

I believe there is no other book in the Bible that invites us into an experience as passionate, personal and transparent as the Psalms. We are given the eloquent expression of every human feeling: hope, remorse, joy and sorrow, confidence and fear, humility and anger, certainty and anxiety. The Psalms goes beyond our intellect and appeal to our emotions as well as our intuition. This book is a guide for life. It is a source of wisdom and insight, lighting our journey through a spiritually dark world (Psalm 119:105). We are given instruction as well as dealing with fundamental issues such as the nature of evil, the meaning of life, and the human struggle to fathom God's ways. God desires to hear our fears, doubts, and sorrows. And the Book of Psalms encourages us to bring our heartache to God who cares.

God is the Supreme God. He is our Global God. He is not just the God of one nation or tribe. He is the Lord over the whole world and God of all nations. He is the God that rules with love, power, justice, and sovereignty. The book of Psalms anticipates both the global message of Jesus (John 3:16-17) and His final rule over all the people of the earth (Revelation 5:9-14). Oh how would our world transform in increasing numbers if people choose to honor God. God alone deserves that level of honor. He is the Most High, the awesome King who rules the earth, every people and nation (Psalm 47:2-3). God loves us and the Psalms call us to maintain a high view of God at all times.

This Great God is calling all people from every "kindred, and tongue, and people, and nation" to come to Him. And as people respond to the call, He forms them into a worldwide body that brings glory to Him. This God is our God! We owe Him a great praise. The psalmist in 48:14 declared that "this God is our God". Psalm 48 tells us why He deserves all the praise because:

- ❖ God is great and deserves immense praise.
- ❖ He lives with His people and provides them with refuge.
- ❖ He is the great King feared around the world.
- ❖ He is steadfastly loving and kind.
- ❖ His praise echoes to the ends of the earth.
- ❖ He is righteous and the source of righteousness.
- ❖ He is just.
- ❖ He is God forever and ever.
- ❖ He guides His people.

In this Psalm, the anticipation of John's end-of-time vision of a new heaven and new earth is seen (Revelation 21-22). God will dwell forever and ever with people from every nation who have come to Him for salvation. Isn't that an awesome hope that God will live among us forever and ever!

King David declared that none could compare to the Lord God. The Psalm offers us a thorough description of the Supreme God. According to Psalm God is:

He is Creator of the World

- ❖ The heavens, the moon, and the stars are the "work of [His] fingers" (8:3).
- ❖ "He commanded, and they were created" (148:5).
- ❖ He "laid the foundations of the earth" (104:5)
- ❖ He gives all creatures life (104:27-30).

He is All Powerful

- ❖ He laughs when human rulers conspire together against Him (2:4).
- ❖ "The voice of the LORD shaketh the wilderness" (29:8).
- ❖ His power causes even His enemies to submit to Him (66:3).

He is All-Wise

- ❖ In His wisdom He created the world (104:24).
- ❖ He is the starting point for wisdom (111:10).
- ❖ He knows everything we do and say (139:2-4).

He is Eternal

- ❖ "From everlasting to everlasting, thou art God" (90:2).
- ❖ "Thou art from everlasting" (93:2).
- ❖ "Thou art the same, and thy years shall have no end" (102:27).

He is Holy

- ❖ "God sitteth upon the throne of his holiness" (47:8).
- ❖ He "is holy" (99.3, 5, 9).
- ❖ "Holy and reverend is his name" (111:9).

He is Good

- ❖ "Good and upright is he LORD" (25:8).
- ❖ "The LORD is good" (100:5).
- ❖ "The LORD is righteous in all his ways" (145:17).

He is Merciful And Forgiving

- ❖ "All the paths of the LORD are mercy and truth" (25:10).

You are God Alone

- He forgives all our iniquities (103:3).
- "His mercy endureth forever" (136:1-26).

He is Faithful

- "They that know thy name will put their trust in thee: for thou, LORD, hast not forsaken them that seek thee" (9:10).
- "He that keepeth thee will not slumber" (121:3).

He is Personally Involved with His Creatures

- He fashions the hearts of people individually (33:16).
- "He causeth the grass to grow for the cattle, and herb for the service of man" (104:14)
- "Thou hast possessed my reins" (139:13).

He is True and Straightforward

- "The judgments of the LORD are true and righteous altogether" (19:9).
- He is the "LORD God of truth" (3:15).
- All His commandments are truth (119:151).

He is Just

- God is a just judge (7:11).
- "He loves righteousness and judgment" (33:5).
- He "executeth justice for the oppressed" (146:7).

The Psalter Also Declares God's:

- Unsearchable greatness (145)
- Preserving power (140)
- Loving kindness (**Psalm 138**)
- Mercy and truth (117)
- Redemptive power (107)
- Wondrous power (105)

- ❖ Glory endures forever (**Psalm 104:31-35**)
- ❖ Marvelous creation (**Psalm 104; 102:25-28**)
- ❖ Everlasting Kingdom (**Psalm 72:17-20; 45**)

I believe the main focus of the Book of Psalms is worship of God. God is worthy of all praise because of who His is, what He has done, and what He will do. His goodness extends throughout all time and eternity. It takes faith to produce confidence in God's power in spite of circumstances, good or bad.

The Psalms or Psalter are really five books in one. Each book or division ends with a doxology or benediction (an ascription of praise to God). It is uncertain why Psalms is divided into five books. Some sources suggest the five divisions are based on the five books of the Torah (teaching) or the first five books of the Bible. Division one is parallel to Genesis: Man and Creation. Division two is parallel to Exodus: Deliverance and Redemption. Division three is parallel to Leviticus: Worship and Sanctuary. Division four is parallel to Numbers: Wilderness and Wandering. Division five is parallel to Deuteronomy: Scripture and Praise.

The first division is from Psalm 1-41 and the doxology is found in Psalm 41:13: *"Blessed be the LORD God of Israel from everlasting, and to everlasting. Amen, and Amen."* The second division is from Psalm 42-72 and the doxology is found in Psalm 72:18-19: *"Blessed be the LORD God, the God of Israel, who only doeth wondrous things. And blessed be his glorious name for ever: and let the whole earth be filled with his glory; Amen, and Amen."* The third division is from Psalm 73-89 and the doxology is found in Psalm 89:52: *"Blessed be the LORD for evermore. Amen, and Amen."* The fourth division is from Psalm 90-106 and the doxology is found in Psalm 106:48: *"Blessed be the LORD God of Israel from everlasting to everlasting: and let all the people say, Amen; Praise ye the LORD"*. The fifth division is from Psalm 107-150 and the doxology is found in Psalm 150:6: *"Let everything that hath breath praise the LORD. Praise ye the*

- ❖ He forgives all our iniquities (103:3).
- ❖ "His mercy endureth forever" (136:1-26).

He is Faithful

- ❖ "They that know thy name will put their trust in thee: for thou, LORD, hast not forsaken them that seek thee" (9:10).
- ❖ "He that keepeth thee will not slumber" (121:3).

He is Personally Involved with His Creatures

- ❖ He fashions the hearts of people individually (33:16).
- ❖ "He causeth the grass to grow for the cattle, and herb for the service of man" (104:14)
- ❖ "Thou hast possessed my reins" (139:13).

He is True and Straightforward

- ❖ "The judgments of the LORD are true and righteous altogether" (19:9).
- ❖ He is the "LORD God of truth" (3:15).
- ❖ All His commandments are truth (119:151).

He is Just

- ❖ God is a just judge (7:11).
- ❖ "He loves righteousness and judgment" (33:5).
- ❖ He "executeth justice for the oppressed" (146:7).

The Psalter Also Declares God's:

- ❖ Unsearchable greatness (145)
- ❖ Preserving power (140)
- ❖ Loving kindness (**Psalm 138**)
- ❖ Mercy and truth (117)
- ❖ Redemptive power (107)
- ❖ Wondrous power (105)

- ❖ Glory endures forever (**Psalm 104:31-35**)
- ❖ Marvelous creation (**Psalm 104; 102:25-28**)
- ❖ Everlasting Kingdom (**Psalm 72:17-20; 45**)

I believe the main focus of the Book of Psalms is worship of God. God is worthy of all praise because of who His is, what He has done, and what He will do. His goodness extends throughout all time and eternity. It takes faith to produce confidence in God's power in spite of circumstances, good or bad.

The Psalms or Psalter are really five books in one. Each book or division ends with a doxology or benediction (an ascription of praise to God). It is uncertain why Psalms is divided into five books. Some sources suggest the five divisions are based on the five books of the Torah (teaching) or the first five books of the Bible. Division one is parallel to Genesis: Man and Creation. Division two is parallel to Exodus: Deliverance and Redemption. Division three is parallel to Leviticus: Worship and Sanctuary. Division four is parallel to Numbers: Wilderness and Wandering. Division five is parallel to Deuteronomy: Scripture and Praise.

The first division is from Psalm 1-41 and the doxology is found in Psalm 41:13: *"Blessed be the LORD God of Israel from everlasting, and to everlasting. Amen, and Amen."* The second division is from Psalm 42-72 and the doxology is found in Psalm 72:18-19: *"Blessed be the LORD God, the God of Israel, who only doeth wondrous things. And blessed be his glorious name for ever: and let the whole earth be filled with his glory; Amen, and Amen."* The third division is from Psalm 73-89 and the doxology is found in Psalm 89:52: *"Blessed be the LORD for evermore. Amen, and Amen."* The fourth division is from Psalm 90-106 and the doxology is found in Psalm 106:48: *"Blessed be the LORD God of Israel from everlasting to everlasting: and let all the people say, Amen; Praise ye the LORD".* The fifth division is from Psalm 107-150 and the doxology is found in Psalm 150:6: *"Let everything that hath breath praise the LORD. Praise ye the*

LORD." Psalm 150 is the grand finale of Psalter! God is worthy of praise and worship because He is the (only) Creator, the (only) Redeemer, and God is Faithful!

In Psalm 2:7, God will declare Him to be His Son. This was fulfilled in Matthew 3:17: *"And lo a voice from heaven, saying, This is my beloved Son, in whom I am well pleased."* In Psalm 8:6, all things will be put under His feet. This was fulfilled in Hebrews 2:8: *"Thou hast put all things in subjection under his feet. For in that he put all in subjection under him, he left nothing that is not put under him. But now we see not yet all things put under him."*

In Psalm 16:10, He will be resurrected from the dead. This was fulfilled in Mark 16:6-7: "And he saith unto them, be not affrighted: Ye seek Jesus of Nazareth, which was crucified: he is risen; he is not here: behold the place where they laid him."

In Psalm 22:1, God will forsake Him in His hour of need. This was fulfilled in Matthew 27:46: "And about the ninth hour Jesus cried with a loud voice, saying, Eli, Eli, lama sabachthani? That is to say, My God, My God, why hast thou forsaken me?"

In Psalm 22:7-8, He will be scorned and mocked. This was fulfilled in Luke 23:35: "And the people stood beholding. And the rulers also with them derided him, saying, He saved others; let him save himself, if he be Christ, the chosen of God."

In Psalm 22:16, His hands and feet will be pierced. This was fulfilled in John 20:25, 27: "The other disciples therefore said unto him, we have seen the Lord. But he said unto them, Except I shall see in his hands the print of the nails and put my finger into the print of the nails, and thrust my hand into his side, I will not believe. Then saith he to Thomas, reach hither thy finger, and behold my hands; and reach hither thy hand, and thrust it into my side: and be not faithless, but believing."

In Psalm 22:18, soldiers will gamble for his clothes. This was fulfilled in Matthew 27:35-36: "And they crucified him, and parted his garments, casting lots: that it might be fulfilled which was spoken by the prophet, they parted my garments among them, and upon my vesture did they cast lots."

In Psalm 34:20, not one of his bones was broken. This was fulfilled in John 19:32, 33, 36: "Then came the soldiers, and break the legs of the first, and of the first, and of the other which was crucified with him. But when they came to Jesus, and saw that he was dead already, they brake not his legs: For these things were done, that the scripture should be fulfilled, A bone of him shall not be broken."

In Psalm 35:11, He will be accused by false witnesses. This was fulfilled in Mark 14:57: *"And there arose certain, and bare false witness against him, saying"*

In Psalm 35:19, He will be hated without cause. This is fulfilled in John 15:25: "But this cometh to pass, that the word might be fulfilled that is written in their law, they hated me without a cause."

In Psalm 40:7-8, He will come to do God's will. This was fulfilled in Hebrews 10:7: "Then said I, Lo, I come (in the volume of the book it is written of me) to do thy will, O God."

In Psalm 41:9 He will be betrayed by a friend. This was fulfilled in Luke 22:47: "And while he yet spake, behold a multitude, and he that was called Judas, one of the twelve, went before them, and drew near unto Jesus to kiss him."

In Psalm 45:6, His throne will be forever. This was fulfilled in Hebrews 1:8: "But unto the Son he saith, Thy throne, O God, is for ever and ever: a scepter of righteousness is the scepter of thy kingdom."

In Psalm 68:18, He will ascend to God's right hand. This was fulfilled in Mark 16:19: "So then after the Lord had spoken unto them, he was received up into heaven, and sat on the right hand of God."

In Psalm 69:9, zeal for God's house will consume Him. This was fulfilled in John 2:17: "And his disciples remembered that it was written, The zeal of thine house hath eaten me up."

In Psalm 69:21, He will be given vinegar and gall to drink. This was fulfilled in Matthew 27:34: "They gave him vinegar to drink mingled with gall: and when he had tasted thereof, he would not drink."

In Psalm 109:4, He will pray for His enemies. This was fulfilled Luke 23:34: *"Then said Jesus, Father, forgive them; for they know not what they do."*

In Psalm 109:8, His betrayer's office will be fulfilled by another. This was fulfilled in Acts 1:20: "For it is written in the book of Psalms, Let his habitation be desolate, and let no man dwell therein: and his bishoprick let another take."

In Psalm 110:1 His enemies will be made subject to Him. This was fulfilled in Matthew 22:44: "The LORD said unto my Lord, Sit thou on my right hand, till I make thine enemies thy footstool?".

In Psalm 110:4, He will be a priest like Melchizedek. This was fulfilled in Hebrews 5:6: "As he saith also in another place, Thou art a priest for ever after the order of Melchisedec."

In Psalm 118:22, He will be the chief cornerstone. This was fulfilled Matthew 21:42: "Jesus saith unto them, Did ye never read in the scriptures, The stone which the builders rejected, the same is become the head of the corner: this is the Lord's doing, and it is marvelous in our eyes?"

In Psalm 118:26, he will come in the name of the Lord. This was fulfilled in Matthew 21:9: "And the multitudes that went before, and that followed, cried, saying Hosanna to the Son of David: Blessed is he that cometh in the name of the Lord; Hosanna in the highest."

God put the finishing touches on our salvation and there are specific messianic prophecies in the Book of Psalms. "It is finished". When Christ died on the cross and rose from the dead, there is nothing to add to it or take away from it. He is seated at the right hand of the throne of God. God sent His Son to finish His plan of salvation for us.

THE WRATH OF GOD: PROVOKING GOD TO ANGER
Chapter Twelve

Today, we hear a lot about God's love, grace, and mercy. However, forget that God is to be feared. He takes sin very seriously; therefore, we should take His holiness very seriously. I know the wrath of God is not a popular subject. We rarely hear messages about it. Which is surprising when the Bible teaches more about the wrath of God than the love of God. It also talks more about hell than of heaven. Always remember that we were all children of wrath by nature (Ephesians 2:2-3). So, the "Wrath of God": God is holy; He totally and completely distances Himself from sin, evil, corruption, and the resulting filth and guilt. He maintains His purity and rejects, fights against, and destroys that which would offend, attack, or undo His holiness and love. Therefore, God's anger and wrath must always be seen in relation to His maintaining and defending His attributes of love and holiness, as well as His righteousness and justice. The emotion or passion that moves God to this maintaining and defending is expressed by the terms "displeasure," "indignation," "anger", and "wrath". A consequence of his wrath is vengeance, punishment, and death. (Baker's Evangelical Dictionary of Biblical Theology).

God is a God of love and a God of judgment and wrath. Yes, we know that God is a God of love, but at the same time He is also a God of justice, righteousness and wrath. The God of wrath is rarely discussed. God's holy character demands that sin be punished. I believe one of our greatest failures is not realizing or recognizing who God is and what His character is like. God is not human. He is Spirit and He is holy. To be holy means to be set apart. In other words, God is set apart from the power, practice, and presence of sin, and is set apart to absolute righteousness and goodness. There is no sin in God and He has nothing to do with sin. Yet, He offers grace and mercy to those who are willing to repent and believe. That is why He sent Jesus into the world. This is the good news of the gospel that Christ died for our sins. God always gives us a choice in our rebellion of wrath and judgment or mercy. God is a good Father.

There is no tension between His wrath and His love. God's moral perfection requires Him to show displeasure (contempt; hate) against anything that is contrary to His moral purpose and holiness and to judge that which rebels against His authority as Creator and Lord (Psalm 103: 8-9; Romans 2:5; 11:22; Hebrews 10:31). His justice will always be administered fairly (Psalm 139:1-5; Proverbs 5:21). God is righteous, meaning that God cannot and will not pass over wrongdoing. He does not look beyond our faults to see our need. He actually has to deal without sin to meet our need. This is why He sent Jesus to be our substitute; our atoning sacrifice.

There are numerous accounts of how God was provoked to anger and had no other choice but to bring judgment. God would send His prophets God's message. He pronounced six woes on Israel and Judah for specific sins. In Isaiah chapter 6, the prophet is commissioned to proclaim, first, a message of condemnation. Judah is saturated with moral and spiritual decay. They were neglecting God as they bowed to ritualism and selfishness. They were guilty of pride and arrogance (9:9, 10), refusing to repent and return to the Lord despite His discipline (9:13), corruption of the nation's leaders (9:15-16), hypocrisy and wickedness (9:17), and unjust laws and policies that robbed the poor (10:1-2). It is repeated four times the phrase: "For all this his anger is not turned away, but his hand is stretched out still" (9:12, 17, 21; 10:4).

The rulers, priests, and the people went about their lives as if god did not matter. When they should have been turning away from sin and corruption and crying out to God for help, they celebrated, violated God's commands and indulged in the wrong attitude. It is very foolish to ignore the times given to us to repent.

Though God is longsuffering, after He watched these sins continue for generations, the Lord promised to allow enemies to destroy the nation's cities (9:11-12), remove its leadership (9:14), destroy the people (9:16-17; 10:4), and trigger famine and civil war. God's wrath may seem to contradict His loving character, but rather we believe it or not it is a part of love (11:5). Remember God in His wisdom, acts to right wrongs and put an end to evil and His anger also brings a better outcome.

The second message from Isaiah was of comfort. After he pronounced Judah's divine condemnation, He comforts them with the promises of God's hope and restoration. We know that foundation of this hope is the sovereignty and majesty of God (40-48). In chapters 40 through 48, 216 of the verses speak of God's greatness and power. God is faithful to His covenant by preserving a godly remnant and promises salvation and deliverance through the coming Messiah. God's people will confess their sins. Peace, prosperity, and justice will prevail and God will make all things new (46:18-19).

Jeremiah was another prophet called to continue to warn God's people to turn back to Him, to give up their idols, to practice piety toward the Lord and integrity toward each other. They perverted the worship of the true God and gave themselves over to spiritual and moral decay. In their refusal to repent, Jeremiah the prophet lists the moral and spiritual causes for their coming catastrophe, but he also proclaimed God's gracious promise of hope and restoration. God always has a remnant and will establish a new covenant. God said that He will put a new covenant by putting His law in their inward parts and write it in their hearts; and will be their God, and they shall be His people (Jeremiah 31:33).

I like the illustration of the two fig baskets in chapter 24 of Jeremiah. One basket had very good figs and the other basket had bad figs. Jeremiah said, "And I said, Figs; the good figs, very good; and the evil, very evil, that cannot be eaten, they are so evil (vs. 3)." Although God allowed the Chaldeans to carry away the "good figs", it was their good. God said, "For I will set mine eyes upon them for good, and I will bring them again to this land: and I will build them, and not pull them down; and I will plant them, and not pluck them up. And I will give them a heart to know me, that I am the LORD; and they shall be my people, and I will be their God: for they shall return unto with their whole heart." (vv.6-7). However, for the evil figs, God delivered them to remove into all the kingdoms of the earth for their hurt, to be a reproach and a proverb, a taunt and a curse (vs.9). God said in verse 10, "And I will send the sword, the famine, and the pestilence, among them, till they be consumed from off the land that I gave unto them and to their fathers."

In the course of the prophet Jeremiah, he announced the Lord's judgement on nine nations. In some way each one contributed to the Israelites' downfall. There are two points I see in as the Lord judged His own, paid their political and spiritual enemies as He preserved and revived His people. First, God's wrath is never without cause. The Lord had definite justification for His wrath: the people of these nations had turned from their Creator to worship and serve false gods. Every nation was guilty and God's holy nature required justice. Second, God's wrath is never without remedy. Just as God had called Judah to repent throughout the years of Jeremiah's ministry, He had also invited these nations to turn to Him and be saved. God provided a gesture of grace. He reached out to them with an amazing promise: He would allow them to learn about Him, just as they had taught the Israelites about their gods. This great God of mercy and grace gave them an opportunity to turn from their worthless idols and serve the one and only true God instead of destroying them for leading His people into sin! But because they refused God's offer of grace, they now faced God's wrath.

There are even psalms that call for the divine judgment of God. These psalms are called imprecatory psalms, meaning to call down a curse. If you have read any these psalms, they seem awfully harsh. However, we must keep in mind that (1) they call for divine justice rather than human vengeance; (2) they ask for God to punish the wicked and thus vindicate His righteousness; (3) they condemn sin; and (4) even Jesus called down a curse on several cities and told His disciples to curse cities that do not receive the gospel message (Matthew 10:14-15).

God's grace is free but it is not cheap. It does not allow us to go on doing whatever we wish, without guilt or consequence. The people of Nineveh are the prime example. The Lord sent Jonah to warn the Ninevites of their impending judgment (Jonah 3). The message was received with dire urgency for the people repented from their wickedness and idolatry with sackcloth and fasting. They cried out to God for mercy, and the Lord stayed His hand.

However, this spiritual awakening was short-lived because Nineveh resumed its cruelties (2 Kings 17:6; 2 Kings 19:35-36). God's wrath fell on Nineveh. The God we serve is "slow to anger and great in power and will not at all acquit the wicked" (Nahum 1:3). The Lord leaves rebellious sinners unpunished for so long. He doesn't turn His back on cruel injustice or ignore prayers of victims. It may not be immediate but it is certain that He will intervene. We can take comfort to know that God will not allow evil to go unchecked forever. Sooner or later, He will deal with people who persist in sin. When He decides it is time, His wrath will come swiftly (Genesis 19:24; 2nd Peter 3:10).

Remember God is always provoked to wrath by serving other gods, wickedness, vanity, and lack of faith in him, etc. Bible has various accounts that verify where God didn't tolerate sin anymore and His wrath was poured out on the trespassers. We read where in Noah's day He brought on the flood that changed the face of the earth. Sodom and Gomorrah provoked God to anger and those cities were destroyed. Even Moses provoked God to anger. I can go on and on but my point is God has not changed (Hebrews 13:8). What provoked God to anger in the Old Testaments can still provoke Him to anger today?

God's wrath is not just demonstrated in the Old Testament but the

New Testament also supports and demonstrates God's wrath. Luke 16:19-31 tells of the story of the rich man and Lazarus. Lazarus died and was carried by the angels to Abraham's side but the rich man also died and was buried and in Hades he was tormented. John 3:36 says, "Whoever believes in the Son has eternal life, but whoever rejects the Son will not see life, for God's wrath remains on Him." The one who believes in the Son will not suffer God's wrath for their sin because the Son took God's wrath upon Himself when He died in our place on the cross (Romans 5:6-11). In other words, those who do not believe in Jesus and reject God with be judged on the day of wrath (Romans 2:5-6).

The wrath of God is a fearsome and terrifying thing. Only those who have been covered by the Blood of Christ, shed on the cross can be assured that God's wrath will never fall on them. Romans 5:9 states, "Since we have now been justified by His blood, how much more shall we be saved from God's wrath through Him." Divine wrath toward sin was poured out on Jesus. He became the propitiation for your sin and mine (Romans 3:25). The outpouring of God's wrath was the greatest act of love this world has ever seen and will ever see. Scripture stated that if I will be lifted up from the earth, I will draw all men's judgment unto me. He is ready to forgive your sins and fill you with the precious Holy Spirit.

It is not too late to seek God while He can be found. I know that God is not lost, but the Bible says, *"You will seek me and find me when you seek me with all your heart."* (Jeremiah 29:13 NIV) The Lord can be found even though we are the ones who are lost. Isaiah 65:1 states, *"I am sought of them that asked not for me; I am found of them that sought me not: I said, behold me, behold me, unto a nation that was not called by my name."* God does not afflict people willingly (See Lamentations 3:31-41).

He is the God of mercy. "It is the LORD's mercies that we are not consumed, because his compassions fail not. They are new every morning: great is thy faithfulness. The LORD is my portion, saith my soul; therefore, will I hope in him. The LORD is good unto them that wait for him, to the soul that seeketh him. It is good that a man should both hope and quietly wait for the salvation of the LORD." Lamentations 3:22-26.

The Lord's judgment always has redemption as its purpose. He wants no one to perish (2nd Peter 3:9), and repentance is available as an alternative to wrath right to the very end. God always gives us a choice of wrath and judgment or of mercy in our rebellion. The choice is ours whether we receive the Lord's grace and mercy or His wrath and fury. We can reject Him and suffer His wrath or we can accept Him by faith and receive the reward of the just. As long as God is God, He cannot and will not overlook sin. The wrath of God is all the more intensified because of the abounding manifestation of His grace, mercy, and love in the gift of His Only Begotten Son, Jesus Christ, as Savior, Lord, and King of the world. Our God is a consuming fire (Hebrews 12:29); "It is a fearful thing to fall into the hands of the living God" (Hebrews 10:31). There is only one thing can save the sinner from the outpouring of God's righteous anger against sin in the day of visitation, namely, faith in the Lord Jesus Christ as Redeemer. Christ is the only one righteous enough to connect a holy God and sinful humanity (1st Timothy 2:5; Hebrews 9:15). Apart from Him, none of us would be free from God's wrath, for all us have sinned (Romans 3:21-26). Therefore, we all have been given the same opportunity for salvation. Because Jesus took on Himself the judgment for our sin, we have access to God.

God does not accept excuses. He will punish those who do not know Him and do not obey the gospel of Jesus Christ. They will be punished with everlasting destruction and shut out from the Presence of the Lord and from the Majesty of His power on the day He comes to be glorified in His holy people (2nd Thessalonians 1:8-10). Every violation and disobedience will receive its just punishment (Hebrews 2:2).

Consequently, God, our Savior, wants all to come to a knowledge of the truth: There is one God and one Mediator between God and

Men, the man Jesus Christ. He gave Himself as a ransom for all men at the right time (1st Timothy 2:3-6). "For God so loved the world He gave His only begotten Son, that whoever believes in him shall not perish but have eternal life", but those who does not believe in Him are already condemned because they did not believe in the name of God's only Son (John 3:16-18). Apostle Paul confirms this in 1st Timothy 4:9, *"That we have put our hope in the living God, who is the Savior of all men, and especially of those who believe* (NIV).

Remember the Lord's return will be like a thief (2nd Peter 3:1; 1st Thessalonians 5:2). We won't know the day or the hour (Matthew 24:36). Therefore, Believers are to live as children of the light. *"God did not appoint us to suffer wrath but to receive salvation through our Lord Jesus Christ."* (1st Thessalonians 5:9). We won't be taken by surprise on That Day because Jesus instructs us to keep watch for His return. So, we keep watch by living a holy and godly life as we look forward to the day of God (2nd Peter 3:11-12). Although the heavens and earth will be destroyed by fire (2nd Peter 3:7,12), the Children of God will be given a new heaven and a new earth, "the home of righteousness" (2nd Peter 3:13). John wrote that he saw a new heaven and a new earth, for the first heaven and the first earth had disappeared. Revelation 21:1-2 states, *"Then I saw a new heaven and a new earth, for the first heaven and earth had passed away, and the sea was no more. I saw the holy city, the new Jerusalem, coming down out of heaven from God, prepared as a bride adorned for her husband."*

It will be a terrible and dreadful thing to hear the Lord say on That Day: "Depart from me." In spite what many may believe, God will never change His standard. The eternal torment of hell is real but it doesn't have to be your reality. So, my plea to those who are unsaved and names are not written in the Lamb's Book of Life is to heed Jesus' warning in Matthew 24:44, *"Be ready, because the Son of Man will come at an hour when you don't expect Him."*

God has provided a way to escape the day of His wrath. That Way is in Jesus Christ, the Way, the Truth, and the Life (John 14:6). By repentance to God and faith in Christ Jesus, you are granted forgiveness of sins, justification, mercy, and salvation with promise of everlasting life (John 3:16; Ephesians 2:8-9). The "thief" is coming, but you can be ready. Don't put it off for this the year of the Lord's favor (Luke 4:19) and today when you hear the voice of the Holy Spirit don't harden your heart (Hebrews 3:15).

The question is will it be Worship or Wrath? Those of us who embraces Christ and His payment for sin can anticipate a celebration that exceeds our greatest expectations. Those who reject the payment for their sin and without Christ can have cause to tremble for their rejection of the offer of deliverance from the wrath to come. It is only in Christ is the hope of escaping wrath.

> "The mercy of God has ordained a way for the love of God to deliver us from the wrath of God without compromising the justice of God."
>
> (John Piper)

God is a God of grace and mercy, yet He is also a God of holiness and wrath. If you have not yet responded to Christ's offer of eternal life, why not make the choice right now?

THE GOODNESS OF GOD
Chapter Thirteen

"Oh give thanks to the LORD, for He is good; for His lovingkindness is everlasting." (Psalm 107:1).

"How great is Thy goodness, which Thou hast stored up for those who fear Thee, which Thou hast wrought for those who take refuge in Thee, before the sons of men!" (Psalm 31:19)

The goodness of God is so very important because it is a foundational truth every Christian should embrace. The goodness of God may then be seen as one facet of His glorious nature and character as well as the overall summation of His nature and character. Moses knew the weight of God's eternal glory as he prayed in Exodus 33:19 for God to show His glory. It states, "Then Moses said, "I pray Thee, show me Thy glory! And HE said, "I Myself will make all My goodness pass before you and will proclaim the name of the LORD before you."

I truly believe that we cannot separate God and His goodness. We cannot have goodness without God and we cannot have God without goodness. As we say in the church: God is good all the time and all the time God is good. God alone is good. God is the source of everything good and perfect. "Whatever is good and perfect is a gift coming down to us from God our Father, who created all the lights in the heavens. He never changes or casts a shifting shadow." (James 1:17 NLT). Isn't it wonderful to know that God does not hold back what is good from His children? Although God is good all in His common grace because He showers blessings on the wicked and the righteous alike (Matthew

5:43-45; Acts 14:16-17), He is particularly good to those who believe in the gospel.

The goodness of God is seen in the gospel. This good news about Jesus Christ and salvation. This great gospel is predicated on the fact that everyone is born a sinner and deserves God's wrath (Romans 1:18:3:23). But the good news that God gives us is that in His goodness He has shown mercy and provided a way to escape His wrath. That way is Jesus Christ! Through His perfect and sinless life, He died on the cross as a sacrifice for the whole world. John 3:16 states, *"For God so loved the world He gave His only begotten son so that whosoever believed on Him shall not perish but have everlasting life."* Nothing else really shows the goodness of God more than in the person of Christ our Lord and Savior. This is the greatest motivation to make us accept what was done for on the cross. In other words, we respond to that goodness by believing that Jesus is the Son of God (John 8:24; Mark 16:16), repenting of (turning away from and turning to God) sins (Luke 13:3; Acts 17:30-31; Acts 2:38) and confessing Christ is Lord by putting faith in Him (Romans 10:9-10).

The Bible tells us that goodness of God leads to repentance (Romans 2:4). As stated previously, through God's goodness and love for us, He gave His only Son for a sacrifice for us. Apostle Paul wrote in 1st Corinthians 5:21, "God made him who had no sin to be sin for us, so that in him we might become the righteousness of God." So, by nature we are not good. Therefore, our old nature has to be changed through Jesus Christ. Our goodness has to come from the source of all goodness and that is God. He urges us to come to repentance which is what His goodness is meant to do. Through His patience, God waits for us to turn to Him. He is a longsuffering God. I often say that although God is longsuffering, don't suffer Him too long.

In other words, don't use God's goodness for an excuse to do evil or stay in evil. Through God's goodness, we have been given grace. We are admonished to not receive His grace in vain (2nd Corinthians 6:1). I believe grace has two sides in a manner of speaking. On the one side, grace brings salvation to all men. Then on the other side, grace teaches us how to deny the old nature and live a life of righteousness. We see this in Titus 2:11, "For the grace of God that bringeth salvation hath appeared to all men, teaching us that, denying ungodliness and worldly lusts, we should live soberly, righteously, and godly, in this present world; looking for that blessed hope, and the glorious appearing of the great God and our Savior Jesus Christ; who gave himself for us, that he might redeem us from all iniquity, and purify unto himself a peculiar people, zealous of good works." As new creations, one of the most crucial things we need to really understand is the grace of God. Why? Because once grace saves us, we must live in and by grace. In other words, grace gives the divine life, power, and ability of God to live a life that is pleasing to God. By faith, we have the God-power flowing and operating in us. It is through the Spirit of Grace we can properly function and operate in whatever He is going to call us to do for Him in this life (Ephesians 4:7; 2nd Corinthians 9:8). God's grace is always sufficient and it is always abounding (2nd Corinthians 12:9; Romans 5:20).

Grace is sovereign! It is so precious and it is a gift from God. We should never take it in vain, abuse or frustrate the Grace of God (Galatians 2:21). We must put off the old nature and put on the new nature, the identity God gives us in Christ. Our will, rights, ambition, agenda, plans, etc. is given up and we do what HE wants us to do. God's grace is calling us to live a life above the kind of life that the world lives or we used to live.

It is such goodness, that we offer up thanksgiving, praise, adoration, reverence, and worship to God. God is so good!!! He loves us. He cares about us. He cares for us. When I think of how good God has been to my family and me, I become so overwhelmed with thanksgiving. It's not that we deserve it, but it is because He is just that GOOD! If I tried to articulate how good God is, I would be rendered speechless! Because I wouldn't know what I could say or do to explain what God has done and how good He is. I can recall with King David in Psalm 103:1-6,8:

Who forgives all your iniquities; who heals all your disease;

Who redeems your life from destruction; who crowns you with loving kindness and tender mercies;

Who satisfies your mouth with good things; so that your youth is renewed like the eagle's.

The LORD executes righteousness and judgment for all that are oppressed.

The LORD is merciful and gracious, slow to anger, and plenteous in mercy."

Therefore, trust in the Goodness of God!

THE DUTY OF MAN TO GOD
Chapter Fourteen

Now all has been heard; here is the conclusion of the matter: Fear God and Keep his commandments, for this is the duty of all mankind. Ecclesiastes 12:13

He has shown you, O mankind, what is good. And what does the LORD require of you but to act justly, to love mercy, and to walk humbly with your God? Micah 6:8

God created man as the crown of all His creation. God created man in His image and after His likeness. Man was created as a being whose very existence is derived from and dependent upon a Creator whom he must acknowledge Yahweh. Man's very purpose and very existence is dependent on God. Man was created for God's glory, that God might manifest Himself and be magnified in, though, and above His creation. "For of him, and through him, and to him, are all things: to whom be glory forever. Amen." (Romans 11:36)

What God requires of us from the beginning has not changed. He still requires us to love Him will all our heart and with all our soul and with all our might (Deuteronomy 6:5). He still requires us to walk in His ways, keep His commandments, hold fast to Him, and serve Him (Joshua 22:5). This cannot be accomplished on our own. The first Adam disobey God and caused separation with God. However, the Last Adam obey God and brought reconciliation with God. Through Jesus' sacrifice we have been given the gift of the Holy Spirit to help us live out our duty to God. When I say duty, I am not talking about repaying God, but as in our faithfulness to Him in every way. God has given us another chance to have a relationship with Him through Jesus Christ. We have to strengthen our relationship to God through prayer, His Word and the Holy Spirit.

Therefore, the Holy Spirit empowers us to understand the Word written about God. He gives us the power to obey the Word. Then He gives us the ability or the grace to declare Jesus Christ as our Lord and to live as His obedient servants. However, the Holy Spirit doesn't do the believing for us. Believing is our duty to God and doing what God says.

LIFE WITHOUT GOD
Chapter Fifteen

There would be no life without God. God is Creator of all. In John 6:66-69, Jesus turned to Peter and asked him if he wanted leave along with the others who were following Jesus. Peter gives a profound answer in verse 69, "Then Simon Peter answered him, Lord, to whom shall we go? Thou has the words to eternal life. We would be in utter darkness without God. He is our life.

So, a life without God there would be no mercy. What is mercy? Mercy can be thought of as compassionate or kindly forbearance shown toward an offender, an enemy, or other person in one's power; compassion, pity, or benevolence (Dictionary.com). A good way for us to understand the meaning of mercy is to see how it relates to grace. When we describe mercy, we say that we don't get what we deserve. Yet with grace, we get what we don't deserve. With mercy the punishment that we deserve is withheld and with grace we are given undeserved favor. In other words, when justice demand punishment mercy became a judge and override justice to withhold that punishment. Whereas grace gives us something we could never have imagined or earned.

What does God's mercy do for us? Well, His mercy prevents God's wrath from consuming us. Jeremiah wrote in Lamentation 3:22, *"It is of the LORD's mercies that we are not consumed, because his compassion fails not."* God's mercy allows us to be forgiven of our sin. Micah 7:18 states, *"Who is a God like you, who pardons sin and forgives the transgression of the remnant of his inheritance? You do not stay angry forever but delight to show mercy."* (NIV) Then God's mercy makes salvation possible. In Titus 3:5 it is written, *"He saved us, not because of righteous things we had done, but because of his mercy. He saved us through the washing of rebirth and renewal by the Holy Spirit."* (NIV) Without mercy a sinner would be destined for eternal torment.

There would be no forgiveness without God. Forgiveness is critical. Each of us needs God's forgiveness. Why? scripture tells us that we all have sinned. Romans 3:23 states, "For all have sinned and fall short of the glory of God." From God's perspective, we were all born in sin and have a sin problem. We are born eternally separated from God. Therefore, we would be utterly lost forever without Him intervening and offering us a chance to be forgiven. Without forgiveness, fellowship with God cannot be established again. Forgiveness removes all barriers between us and God. Without God there would be no forgiveness at all. We are told that without the Shedding of blood there would be no forgiveness of sin (Hebrew 9:22).

Hope is very important living in this fallen world, but without God there is no hope. The scripture tells us that we were once separated from Christ and we had no hope without God in the world (Ephesians 2:12). But thanks to God, we have been given an anchor for our hope and our hope is anchored in Christ (Hebrews 6:19). It is through hope we have eternal life and we are heirs (Titus 1:1-2; Titus 3:7). In fact, we have been born again to a living hope through the resurrection of Jesus Christ from the dead (1st Peter 1:3). And we know that this hope is unseen. It is what Hebrews 11:1 says about hope: Now faith is the assurance of things hoped for, the evidence of things not seen. I would say hope is very important and we cannot have hope without God.

These are just a few, but can you imagine a world without God. A world without God is a scary thought. For me, it is an impossible scenario. Without God there would be no life. Our life would have no meaning. People would live for themselves and would do anything and everything to get what they wanted, without regard for others. A world without God would be dark and the void of His Light. Everyone not born-again has no hope without God. The Bible teaches us about being separated from God and being in utter darkness and eternal separation for Him.

Scripture is very clear that there are only two destinations for our soul following death or the return of Christ (Matthew 25:34, 41, 46; Luke 16:22-23). The righteous will inherit eternal life. So, the only way to be declared righteous before God is through faith in the Jesus Christ (John 3:16-18; Romans 10:9). The souls of the righteous will be in the presence of God (Luke 23:43; 2 Corinthians 5:8; Philippians 1:23). However, those who reject salvation and die in their sin will receive everlasting punishment (2nd Thessalonians 1:8-9). The Bible describes this punishment in various ways: a lake of fire (Luke 16:24; Revelation 20:14-15), outer darkness (Matthew 8:12), and a prison (1st Peter 3:19).

After leaving this earth, there is no more chances to repent and turn to God and put faith in Jesus Christ. In Hebrews 9:27, it is made clear that everyone dies physically and, after that, comes the judgment. 2nd Thessalonians 1:8-9 states, *"He will punish those who do not know God and do not obey the gospel of Jesus Christ, Lord and Savior. They will be punished with everlasting destruction and shut out from the presence of the Lord and from the glory of his might."* Because God is the source of everything good, to be without God is to forfeit all exposure to anything good. Those in hell have forever lost the chance to see God's face and be in His light (1st John 1:5), His love (1st John 4:8), His joy (Matthew 25:23), and His peace (Ephesians 2:14).

GOD'S KINGDOM
Chapter Sixteen

The Kingdom speaks of God Himself, the Eternal Kingdom. God's Kingdom as revealed in Scripture, presents the purpose, process, and final realization of the divine government in the earth. It is the power of God in action as His rule, reign and authority. We especially see the objective is the heart of the Kingdom prayer as taught by Jesus to His disciples: Thy kingdom come. Thy will be done in earth as it is in heaven (Matthew 6:9). God's Kingdom is where He Reigns and Rules. It is His Royalty. 1st Corinthians 15:24-28 states, *"Then cometh the end, when he shall have delivered up the Kingdom of God, even the Father; when he shall have put down all rule and authority and power. For he must reign, till he hath put all things under his feet. But when he saith all things are put under him, it is manifest that he is excepted, which did put all things under him. And when all things shall be subdued unto him, then shall the Son also himself be subject unto him that put all things under him, that God may be all in all."* The reestablishment of the authority of God is first mentioned in Genesis 3:15, where it is stated that the Seed of the woman should bruise the head of Satan.

The Gospel of the Kingdom is the good news message of repentance, redemption and restoration offered by God to all who will receive Christ by faith. Those who accept this offer become part of His eternal Kingdom (John 1:12). Those who choose to remain in their sin cannot be a part of this Kingdom (1st Corinthians 6:9-10; Galatians 5:19-21). Although grace makes this offer available to any and everyone who will receive it, Jesus warned that it would be very difficult to enter His Kingdom and few would do so (Matthew 7:14).

The Gospel of the Kingdom is the news that there is freedom

from our slavery to sin (decay, destruction, ruin) if we will repent and turn to God (Romans 6:18-19). Our Redeemer has come, but it is difficult to enter God's Kingdom, not because God requires impossible standards for us, but because we do not want to repent and change. We do not want to make the turn towards God that is necessary. We tend to love the darkness more than the Light (John 3:19). Many would rather cling to their old sinful identities than allow Jesus to create them anew (2nd Corinthians 5:17).

Those who receive the Gospel of the Kingdom becomes a citizen and is freed from bondage to this world (Galatians 4:3-9). 2nd Corinthians 5:20 refers to God's children as "Ambassadors" for our heavenly Father. Just as an earthly foreign ambassador retains their national identity when representing their country in another, the spiritual ambassadors of God's Kingdom owe their allegiance to God even as they reside in this world. Remember once we have been born from above, we are now new creations and we are in this world but not of this world. Therefore, we must follow our heavenly Father's code of conduct while sojourners on earth. Essentially, we need not be conformed to this world's habits, values, and lifestyles, because this is not our home (Romans 12:1-2; 1st John 2:15-17).

Jesus said, *"My Kingdom is not of this world."* (John 18:36). So, although we must live here until God calls us home, we are not to live for ourselves or according to this world's value system. Those who have been bought by the Blood of Jesus have been given the right to live according to God's value system. Citizens of the Kingdom of God live here on assignment from our Father the King of Glory. Living with a Kingdom mindset empowers us to make wiser decisions as we invest our lives in advancing the gospel of the Kingdom.

The Church is mandated to advance the Kingdom here in the earth. The book of Acts gives us a clear example of how to advance the Kingdom. These first century disciples followed in the footsteps of Christ Himself. And what is that example? Acts 10:38 answers this question: *"How God anointed Jesus of Nazareth with the Holy Spirit and with power. He went about doing good and healing all who were oppressed by the devil, for God was with him."* It is not just preaching and teaching. *"For the Kingdom of God is not just a lot of talk; it is living by God's power"* (1st Corinthians 4:20 NLT). Paul wrote that his speech and his preaching was not with enticing words of human wisdom, but in the manifestation of the Spirit and of power (1st Corinthians 2:4). Additionally, the Kingdom of God is righteousness, peace, and joy in the Holy Spirit (Romans 14:17).

When the Disciples did what Jesus did and said what Jesus said, the church grew exponentially! When we look at Acts chapter 2, we see how the church grew. After Peter preached under the power of the Holy Spirit, about 3,000 souls were added to them (vs. 41). Then verses 42 – 47 gives the practices of the early church.

"And they continued stedfastly in the apostles' doctrine (the teaching of Jesus" and fellowship, and in breaking of bread, and in prayers. And fear came upon every soul: and many wonders and signs were done by the apostles. And all that believed were together and had all things in common; and sold their possessions and goods, and parted them to all, as every man had need. And they, continuing daily with one accord in the temple, and breaking bread from house to house, did eat their meat with gladness and singleness of heart, Praising God, and having favour with all the people. And the Lord added to the church daily such as should be saved."

We see that the church is not a building made of bricks and mortar, but it is the company or congregation of believing souls who have been born again from above (John 3:3,5) and baptized into the body of Christ. These verses record the first meeting of the first local church. Often the question arises about the decrease in attendance. There are those who ask what the church can do to increase their numbers. My answer to them is follow the example of the first century church and the Lord will add to your number. The church is a divine institution because He does the adding to the Church those who are being saved. In fact, no human can add to the Church; it is purely the Lord's doing. Christ is the Door we enter in. He is the Way, the Truth and the Life. No one can get to the God the Father except they come through Christ and God does the drawing (John 14:6; John 6:44). In other words, only the Lord can do the work of building His church (upon this Rock I build my church and the gates of hell will not prevail against it); only Christ can add to the Church so that it increases and multiplies and become stronger each day.

In advancing the Kingdom of God, the Church is the Body of Christ and He works through His Body, that is to say, through the members of the Church, through Christians who are members of the Church, to build it up and extend it through the witness of Christ through the great commission (Matthew 28:16-20). From verse 41 to 47 in that 2nd Chapter we see the following characteristics of the early church left for us as an example. In verse 41, they were soundly converted. In verse 41, they were openly committed. In verse 42, they were truly obedient. In verse 44, they were obviously gloriously united. In verses 46-47, they were obviously consistent. Remember, God has already established a way for the church to advance the Kingdom. So, we aren't called to build the Kingdom of God but to advance what has already been established. We can't extend God's reign, but we can help people understand what it's like to live under His reign. We do that by our words, our actions, and our love for one another (John 13:34-35). We have been called as Ambassadors of Christ as though God is making His appeal through us.

GOD'S HEART FOR THE WORLD
Chapter Seventeen

God so love the world he gave his only begotten son...
(John 3:16)

Man became a living being after God blew into his nostrils the breath of life (Genesis 2:7). After the rebellion of Adam and Eve, God shows His heart towards them like a loving Father. It was God who pursued them in the Garden and dressed them with the appropriate clothes. Though they died spiritually immediately and began to die physically, God had humanity's redemption in mind when He declared in Genesis 3:15, *"And I will put enmity between thee and the woman, and between thy seed and her seed; it shall bruise thy head, and thou shalt bruise his heel."* It was God's heart for the World to be rescued and be reconciled to Him in love.

God comes looking for us even in our sinful state for while we were still sinners Christ died for us (Romans 5:8). He wants to get back into relationship with us. He wants to reconcile us back to Himself. Through the Blood of Christ, we are to do just that "be reconciled to God" (2nd Corinthians 5:20). It should be a great comfort to everyone that this loving God wants us for Himself. He comes looking for us and finds us. Then He calls us to a personal relationship with Him. We love Him because He first loved us. (1st John 4:19).

I believe God shows us His heart in 2nd Corinthians 13:14, *"The grace of the Lord Jesus Christ, and the love of God, and the communion of the Holy Spirit be with you all. Amen."* The Father's heart towards us is love. It makes me sad when I hear people talk about how unworthy they are when in fact God sees us through the heart of grace. His desire is to bless us regardless of how unworthy we see ourselves; because of the agape love that the Father has for us. This kind of love loves us no matter what. This love does not decrease or increase of what we do. There is nothing we can do that will cause Him to love us any less or more than He already does. The heart of God towards us is grace, love, and fellowship. Because of the heart of God for the world, He sent His Son to rescue us. Jesus showed us that God is personal, like a wise, loving, tender, and watchful Father.

As we grow spiritually, it is God's desire that we increasingly know the love He has for us as Father and His Father-heart in our everyday life. I believe that God is our Father is one of the great truths of the Bible and declaration each born again believer can make. We are taught of our Father's amazing closeness, intimacy, warmth and tenderness towards His children. As we accept Christ, we become the sons of God. John 1:12 states, *"But as many as received him, to them gave he power to become the sons of God, even to them that believe on his name."* The term sons of God means that we now have the mind of God. The love of God is expressed in Jesus Christ as our Savior and Lord, who became our substitute. There was a price to pay but we could not pay it. Both Roman 6:23 and Ezekiel 18:20 states that sinners have to die. This is what Romans 6:23 states, *"The wages of sin is death."* Ezekiel states, *"The soul who sins must die."* God's eternal purpose was accomplished in Christ. It is in Him and through faith in Him we can draw near to God with freedom and confidence (Ephesians 3:11-12). As born-again believers, as the Spirit strengthens us in the inner man, Christ dwells in our hearts through faith. We are rooted and established in the love of the Father's heart. This is the gospel that comes by Jesus Christ from God and it is the power of God unto salvation.

I believe God expects those who are now His born from above to operate in the discipline of His love. The same love that allowed Him to be pleased to make Jesus suffer for our sins. Through His mercy and great love, we who were once dead in our trespasses and sins, God has provided salvation for us. Therefore, we know that love is from God and everyone who loves is born of God and knows God (1st John 4:7). This love is poured in our hearts by the Holy Spirit (Romans 5:5). Without this divine pouring, we can never love like God. God's love is holy and His love seeks to make us holy. God cannot accept us any other way. I know many people think God's love is such that He accepts us just as we are but this is not true. We are only accepted by God in Christ. God cannot and will not accept our sin. It is said that God will meet us where we are but He won't leave us that way. Through His love He has provided a way for each of us to be accepted by Him and that is by the Blood of Jesus. Through the praise of the glory of His grace, God has made us accepted in the Beloved (Ephesians 1:6). Through the heart of the Father, God has made all Believers born from above acceptable in His sight. In other words, God does not accept us on what we say or what we do. He does not accept us for what we have or what we don't have. It is through Christ's finished sacrifice on the cross. God accepts us because we are IN CHRIST.

God's love must be manifested in us and through us. There is no other way that this world that we belong to God. In fact, Jesus commanded us to love one another. In John 13:34-35 He said, *"A new commandment I give unto you, that ye love one another; as I have loved you, that ye also love one another. By this all men will know that you are My disciples, if you love one another."* Love is the distinguishing mark of being a follower of Christ. God has made it so that we are a group identified by one thing: LOVE. This love God wants displayed through every believer is unlike the *"love"* generated by the flesh, which can be selfish, egotistical, unforgiving, insincere, etc. However, the love given to us in our hearts by the Holy Spirit gives our new hearts the capacity to love like Christ loves, for we know a love that is unconditional, sacrificial, forgiving, eternal, and holy. We show that we love God when we obey His command.

As we have the Father's heart revealed to us more and more, we realize that He first loved us. When we encounter the Father's heart our lives will never be the same. Jesus came to show us the Father's heart towards us. Jesus said that once we know Him, we also know the Father (John 14:7). Our hearts were created with a longing for the assurance that we are enjoyed by the Father. Our life is transformed as we see how the Father feels about us in our weakness. He enjoys us now. He loves us as we grow and mature in His love. And we are to love God back. We are to adore Him. We are to believe Him. As His adopted children, we have access to the His heart. We cry Abba, Father (Romans 8:15). Through the revelation of the Father's heart we are empowered to endure difficulty and to reject the enemy's accusations and condemnation about us. Therefore, we experience deliverance and wholeness as we are equipped to walk out this fullness of our destiny in this life.

Remember that knowing the heart of the Father is the source of great peace and great power in our walk as Believer. God loves us and is calling you and me to a great intimacy; to a deeper knowledge of who He is and His ways; to love Him with all our heart, soul, mind and strength. Romans 8:35 tells us, *"Who could ever separate us from the endless love of God's Anointed One? Absolutely no one! For nothing in the universe has the power to diminish his love toward us. Troubles, pressures, and problems are unable to come between us and heaven's love. What about persecutions, deprivations, dangers, and death threats? No, for they are all impotent to hinder omnipotent love."* (TPT) God loves us with an everlasting love and has drawn us with unfailing kindness (Jeremiah 31:3). He has placed a banner of love over us. God rejoices over us with singing because He has dressed us in the garments of salvation and the robe of righteousness (Zephaniah 3:17; Isaiah 61:10). We are precious in His sight.

Prayer

Father, come and indwell my heart with Your loving Presence. Heal my hurts; cast out my anxious thoughts. Let Your peace that passes all understanding reign in my heart and over my life. Fill me with Your wonderful Spirit so that I might live each day knowing that Your heart is always towards me because I am accepted in the Beloved. I have tasted and seen that You are good. Amen.

CHOOSE GOD AND LIVE: THE CHOICE IS YOURS
Chapter Eighteen

"I call heaven and earth to record this day against you, that I have set before you life and death, blessing and cursing: therefore choose life, that both thou and thy seed may live:" Deuteronomy 30:19

God has given us the conscious ability to choose whether or not we will love Him. This freedom that we have to choose is the most wonderful and the most precious gift we have been given. God does not make us love Him or force us to choose Him. This is a choice that no one can make for us. Life or death, it's up to us. We have been given free will by our Creator, God. Every choice we make is an exercise of this freedom. What we choose to believe is what becomes our reality.

The reality is that God has made it possible for each of us to choose life. We can choose life because of God's Gospel plan of salvation (GPS). In choosing life, you must first understand why you need to be saved. Simply, you need to be saved because you have sinned. The Bibles teaches that everyone has sinned (Ecclesiastes 7:20; Romans 3:23; 1st John 1:8). Sin entails rebellion and disobedience against God. It dishonors God. Because God is holy and just, He cannot allow sin to go unpunished. Therefore, the punishment for sin is death (Romans 6:23) and eternal separation from God (Revelation 20:11-15). Essentially, without God's GPS, eternal death is the destiny of every human being.

The Gospel that comes by Jesus Christ from God is the power of God unto salvation. It is God who has saved us and called us to a holy life. Not because of His own purpose and grace (2nd Timothy 1:8-9). Grace and truth came through Jesus Christ (John 1:17). Before the start of time, grace has been given to us in Christ Jesus. And we know by God's Word, that the grace of God that brings salvation has appeared to all men (Titus 2:11). The grace of God gives us the strength to choose life. We can say *"no"* to all ungodliness and worldly lusts. Grace helps us to live self-controlled, upright and godly lives (Titus 2:12).

Jesus is our High Priest once and for all. God designated Him to be High Priest in order of Melchizedek (Hebrews 5:10). Jesus who is the radiance of God's glory and the exact representation of His being provided purification for our sins and sins for the whole world. After which He sat down at the right hand of God, the Majesty in Heaven (Hebrews 1:3). He is our merciful and faithful High Priest in service to God (Hebrews 2:17). He serves in the sanctuary, the true tabernacle set up by the Lord not by man (Hebrews 8:1). He is the faithful son over God's house (Hebrews 3:6). It is a great and awesome thing to be granted the right to approach the throne of Grace with confidence to get what we need. Hebrews 4:16 states, *"Let us then approach the throne of grace with confidence so that we may receive mercy and find grace to help us in our time of need."*

As our eternal High Priest, Jesus only had to offer up a sacrifice once for all when He sacrificed Himself (Hebrews 6:27), Unlike the high priest selected from among men. They were subject to weakness and had to offer sacrifices for his own sins every year. Jesus knew no sin. He is holy, blameless, pure, set apart from sinners and exalted above the heavens (Hebrews 6:26). The priests who were appointed by the law were weak but Jesus was appointed by the oath that was spoken by God and has been made perfect forever (Hebrews 7:28).

It is through Jesus a better hope is introduced because we can draw near to God. He is a better hope because Jesus lives forever and has a permanent priesthood (Hebrews 7:23-24). And the Bible tells us, *"Therefore, He is able to save completely those who come to God through Him, because He always lives to intercede for them."* (Hebrews 7:25).

Because of the great sacrifice and price made for the salvation of the world, those in the twice born family should no longer live as the unsaved/unconverted. For the carnal mind is futile in their thinking. Their understanding is darkened and they are separated from the life of God. A heart that remains hardened is still ignorant and in darkness. The old nature is corrupted by its deceitful desires. Therefore, we are instructed to put off the old man; the old self, the sinful nature and be made new in our minds and our thinking. Then put on the new nature; the new self, which have been created to be like God in true righteousness and holiness. True righteousness comes from the imputed righteousness of Christ.

We thank God our Father, who has qualified us for the heritance in the Kingdom of Light. He has rescued us from the dominion of darkness and placed us in the Kingdom of His beloved Son, Jesus (Colossian 1:12-13). Because it is in Christ Jesus our Lord that we have redemption. Our sins have not only been forgiven but our sins have been done away with. We are justified, just as if we never sinned. We are no longer separated from God. Our eternal Lord is the Savior, who transformed sinful people into children of God.

Jesus Christ is the natural heir and God said, *"You are my Son; today I have become your Father."* (Hebrews 5:5; Psalm 2:7). And we are God's adopted children through Jesus Christ (Ephesians 1:5). Therefore, what belongs to Jesus also belongs to us. Jesus gives us His glory (John 17:22), His riches (2nd Corinthians 8:9), and all things (Hebrews 1:2). We have the same welcome mat as Jesus; we are accepted in the Beloved (Ephesians 1:6). God took us from being outcasted orphans in this world and by the blood of Christ we have been made part of His family through faith in Jesus (Ephesians 2:13). We were purchased with the blood of the Lamb for God. We have been made to be a Kingdom and priests to serve our God – as we reign on the earth (Revelation 5:9-10).

If you were to die today, do you know for sure you would go to Heaven? Will you hear Jesus say, *"go to my right"* or *"go to my left"*? If you haven't received God's plan of salvation, now is the time to place your faith in Jesus as your savior. Change your mind from embracing sin and rejecting God to Rejecting sin and embracing God through Jesus Christ. Fully trust in the sacrifice of Jesus as the perfect and complete payment for your sins. Once you do this, you are now saved, your sins will be forgiven, and you will spend eternity with the LORD. There is no other decision as important as the choice of life. Place your faith in Jesus Christ as your Savior and Lord, TODAY!

"The day you hear my voice harden not you heart."
(Hebrews 3:15)

CONCLUSION

The big question is what does the fact of the existence of God means to us as human beings?

First, the knowledge of the existence of God means that man is put here by design. It means that while all God's creatures have purpose, due to man's particular uniqueness among the creatures of God, man has special purpose and meaning. We are not merely the product of time plus chance or some impersonal force. We are each the result of a personal God who created us for Himself with meaning and purpose. But the details of this purpose are found only in the Bible, God's special revelation of Himself. Creation of course cannot and does not reveal this. Creation's primary role is to give man the evidence and basis for God-consciousness (Ps. 19:1-6; Rom. 1:18-20).

Second, the knowledge of God means responsibility. The fact that there is a supreme and perfect being, a divine sovereign who created us for His purposes, means that we are each responsible to Him for the way we live and for what we do with the life He has given us.

Third, the knowledge of God's existence means that we have the responsibility to search and seek to know God personally and intimately, to be thankful, and to worship Him accordingly (Rom. 1:18-23). The facts are, however, that man in his fallen state does not search for God, at least not on his own (Rom. 3:11). But in His grace, God constantly works to draw men to Himself (see John 1:9; 6:44; 7:17; 12:32; Acts 17:27-28; Rom. 2:4; Jer. 29:13; 2nd Chron. 15:2, 4).

Doxology
33 Oh, the depth of the riches of the wisdom and
knowledge of God!
How unsearchable his judgments,
and his paths beyond tracing out!
34 "Who has known the mind of the Lord?
Or who has been his counselor?"
35 "Who has ever given to God,
that God should repay them?"
36 For from him and through him and for him are
all things.
To him be the glory forever! Amen.

FROM THE AUTHOR

Plainly, I do what I do with passion and humility by the grace of God because I am a daughter-servant of God and of Jesus Christ for the faith of God's elect and the knowledge of the truth that leads to godliness. It is no point in proclaiming this gospel without it being able to produce godliness in the lives of those who accept it. I believe one of the greatest abominations a person can make before God is to profess faith in Christ while at the same time living a life of disobedience to Him and His Word.

It is through the grace of God that brings salvation to all men. This grace of God teaches us to *"say no to ungodliness and worldly passions, and to live self-controlled, upright and godly lives in this present age, while we wait for the blessed hope – the glorious appearing of our great God and Savior, Jesus Christ, who gave himself for us to redeem us from all wickedness and to purify for himself a people that are his very own, eager to do what is good."* (Titus 2:11-14 NIV). Remember that the knowledge of Christ must affect a transformation in us that our testimony will *"adorn the doctrine of God"* (Titus 2:10). If we are to adorn the doctrine, the doctrine must also adorn us.

There is no other so-called god, no superpower on earth, no human being who can match God's sovereignty, authority, or power. The bible declares that God alone can say what will happen in the future because He alone is God. He is just and the Savior and He is ready to save all people of the world. He is the source of all righteousness and He is the one to whom every knee will ultimately bow. He is an awesome God who deserves and demands our complete devotion, reverence, obedience, and faithfulness.
God's Grace Be with You All,

Dr. Mary J. Bryant

www.ingramcontent.com/pod-product-compliance
Lightning Source LLC
Chambersburg PA
CBHW021957290426
44108CB00012B/1105